The gift of a renewed diaconate

The gift of a renewed diaconate

and the contribution of
British Methodism

David Clark

FastPrint Publishing

The Gift of a Renewed Diaconate

First Published in 2018 by FastPrint Publishing
Peterborough, England.

A CIP catalogue record for this book is available
from the British Library

Paperback ISBN 978-178456-611-1

Printed and bound in England by
www.printondemand-worldwide.com

www.fast-print.net/bookshop

Contents

**To my colleagues in
the Methodist Diaconal Order**

Foreword

This set of papers has been produced because of my conviction that the gradual emergence worldwide of a renewed diaconate is one of God's gifts to the church of the future. I believe the acceptance of that gift, and obedience to what it entails, will not only transform our understanding of ordained leadership, but of the place of the people of God in the life and mission of church. I see a renewed diaconate as a catalyst for the emergence of the church to come, that which I call 'the diaconal church'[1].

My conviction that the coming into being of a renewed diaconate opens up a new vision of church has come late on in my ministry. For some forty years I was a presbyter in the British Methodist Church. For eleven of those years I served as a circuit minister, in Sheffield and inner London. In part, because of my disillusionment with the failure of the Anglican-Methodist scheme for unity in the 'sixties and, in part, because of my belief in the transformative power of education, I opted to become a minister in secular employment on the staff of Westhill College, Birmingham, a Free Church college and member of the Selly Oak Federation of Colleges. My role at Westhill was the training of youth and community workers, social workers, probation officers and community educators. However, alongside my paid employment, Westhill offered me the opportunity to set up a range of innovative projects[2] which sought to reflect something of the form and mission of the church to come.

During my last few years at Westhill, I came into close contact with the Methodist Diaconal Order, whose headquarters were then located in Birmingham. As a result, I began to realize that, since moving to Birmingham and working on the boundary of church and society, most of my ministry had been diaconal rather than presbyteral. Thus, in 2005, and soon after retirement, with the permission of the Methodist Church and warm encouragement of the then Warden of the Methodist

---

[1] Clark (2005, 2008, 2016)
[2] Clark (1984, 1987, 1997, 2005, 2012)

Diaconal Order, I 'ended' my ministry as a presbyter and became a deacon.[1] It is a move that has enriched my ministry, and deepened my understanding and appreciation of the life and work of the Order.

Well over a decade as a deacon has confirmed my early belief that the Methodist Diaconal Order is a pioneering expression of the nature and form of diaconal ministry. This is for a number of reasons. First, the Order has a strong sense of commitment to working with those beyond the walls of the gathered church, not least the disadvantaged and marginalized. Second, as a religious order, bonded closely together by its Rule of Life, it has a deep sense of community and zest for living the faith. Third, it is part of a church which openly acknowledges deacons and presbyters as equal orders of ministry.

In 2013, the Methodist Conference commissioned a wide-ranging review of the theology and ecclesiology underpinning the Methodist Diaconal Order and its place within Methodism and the universal church, which I describe more fully in the Introduction to this book. This review was set up because, although the Methodist Conference had, in 1993, accepted the Methodist Diaconal Order as both an order of ministry and a religious order, it had become aware that it was an affirmation taken without as full an understanding of the theological and ecclesiological underpinning of diaconal ministry as might be desired. The Methodist Conference also wanted to be clearer as to the relationship of its diaconal order to its presbyteral order, as well as to the Methodist Church as a whole. That review has had a long and variable history. However, it is to be hoped that, when it is completed (scheduled for 2019), a compelling vision of what the gift of a renewed diaconate would mean to Methodism and the wider church will emerge.

For some years before Methodism commissioned this review, the potential of a renewed diaconate to transform the nature of church leadership had been gaining momentum on the world stage, as developments in North America in particular show. The twenty-second Assembly of DIAKONIA, the worldwide association of diaconal networks, held in Chicago in 2017, explored with energy and excitement diaconal 'visions for the future'. Over the past year or two, a number of high profile leaders within the Church of England, a church for

---

[1] The Methodist Diaconal Order only accepted men after it re-opened in 1986.

centuries wedded to the concept of a transitional diaconate, and until recently showing little interest in a permanent diaconate, have begun to speak out about the latter's potential for enhancing the life and mission of their own church.

British Methodism, through the Methodist Diaconal Order, has hitherto gone a long way towards establishing a unique and dynamic model of the permanent diaconate. These papers have been written to offer a vision, not only in principle but also in practice, of what more British Methodism might contribute to furthering the creation of a renewed diaconate. The Methodist Church has the privilege of being endowed with many features of the church to come, the diaconal church. I am passionate that we as Methodists add to these features an awareness of and commitment to embracing what a renewed diaconate can offer both to our own ministry and mission, and to that of the universal church.

David Clark
Bakewell
September 2018

Introduction

The papers in this book were written over the past two years (2016 to 2018), initially to offer my view of how the British Methodist Church should respond to an initiative taken by the Methodist Conference of 2013. That initiative was to commission an exploration of the contribution of the Methodist Diaconal Order (MDO)[1] to the life and work of Methodism and the wider church. The exact wording of the 2013 Conference resolution was as follows:

> The British Methodist Conference commissions its Faith and Order Committee 'to undertake work on the theology and ecclesiology underpinning the Methodist Diaconal Order, its place within the British Connexion[2] and its place within the universal church'.

The immediate reason for this commission was some confusion then existing within the Methodist Church as to the role and status of the Warden of the MDO in relation to other leadership offices, such as Chairs of District. However, this more limited concern was eventually replaced by a desire to explore more thoroughly the theological and ecclesiolgical underpinning of the MDO, and its contribution to British Methodism and the wider church.

It is doubtful whether the Methodist Conference of 2013 fully understood the demanding nature of such a commission. However, it had grasped that the coming into being of the Methodist Diaconal Order heralded the emergence of a new and dynamic form of leadership within the life of the church, of significance not only to Methodism

---

[1] In this book the initials MDO will frequently be used to refer to the Methodist Diaconal Order.

[2] Ecclesiologically, the Methodist Church regards itself as a communal body made up of an extended network of districts, circuits, local churches and related groups and organizations, which make up what it calls 'the Connexion'. Oversight and authority lies with its annual Conference, an elected body consisting of presbyters, deacons and laity. When presbyters and deacons are ordained, they are also 'received into Full Connexion'.

but to 'the universal church'. Here British Methodism was reflecting the growing realization worldwide that a renewed diaconate could well be a gift to the church to come of immense importance in shaping its leadership and empowering its mission.

Methodism's Faith and Order Committee, alongside its many other commitments, sought to respond to this commission as faithfully as it could. However, it was not until May 2016 that it was able to produce an 'Interim Report'[1]. This report was well informed on history but limited in any vision of a renewed diaconate. In particular, it made little reference to the discussions going on across many denominations worldwide concerning the potential of a renewed diaconate for reshaping the ministry and mission of the universal church. No other report from the Faith and Order Committee is scheduled to appear until the Methodist Conference of 2019.

In September 2016, I produced a detailed response to the Interim Report which was circulated to the Faith and Order Committee and a number of other bodies and individuals[2]. Over subsequent months, I reflected on and discussed with numerous diaconal colleagues the issues raised by the Conference's commission of 2013. The outcome has been the papers published in this book. These relate not only to issues raised in the Interim Report but to two other reports (see below).

These papers have been written in the context of a groundswell of interest, especially in the West, and across all denominations, in the potential of a renewed diaconate to bring new inspiration and dynamism to the mission of the church. That groundswell has informed and energized my own thinking and has contributed a great deal to what has been written here. How to realize the potential of a renewed diaconate is not only an immensely important concern for British Methodism, but for every other church as well.

I hope, therefore, that these papers will be of interest not only to my diaconal colleagues and to Methodism, but to those in other

---

[1] www.methodist.org.uk/.../33-theology-and-ecclesiology-underpinning-the-diaconate

[2] My response to the Faith and Order Committee's Interim Report is not included in this book as most of the points made are covered in the papers published here. However, that response is available from: david@clark58.eclipse.co.uk

denominations excited by the potential of a renewed diaconate for reshaping the ministry and mission of the church to come. I especially hope that they will stimulate lively debate about the nature of a renewed diaconate and how it might enrich the leadership of that which I call 'the diaconal church'.

A brief historical background to the Methodist Diaconal Order

To understand many issues addressed and points made in these papers, a short history of how the Methodist Diaconal Order came into being is needed.[1]

Beginnings

The life and work of the Methodist Diaconal Order had its origins in the emergence of a number of Methodist deaconess associations in the late nineteenth century. As with many other deaconess organizations of this era, the Methodist associations came into being to meet the acute social needs of rapidly growing cities with their squalid living conditions and totally inadequate medical care, welfare provision and education for the poor.

In 1869, the Rev Thomas Bowman Stephenson founded the Children's Home (later called the National Children's Home and Orphanage and, more recently, Action for Children). He was greatly influenced by the work of Pastor Theodore Fliedner, the founder of a Lutheran deaconess community in 1836 in Kaiserswerth, Germany. In 1878, Bowman recruited women to work for the Children's Home as Sisters of the Children. This initiative triggered the idea of an order of women employed in three main fields: moral and spiritual education; ministry to the sick; and evangelism.

In 1890, Stephenson built on these foundations to set up the Wesley Deaconess Order, a body distinct from the sisters working for the Children's Home. The work developed rapidly. In 1894 the first deaconess was sent to work in South Africa, the beginning of a long tradition of overseas service by the Order. In 1901 deaconesses were officially 'recognized' as a lay form of ministry by the Wesleyan

---

[1] Much of the material in this section first appeared in Clark (2016), pp.173-177

3

Methodist Conference. In 1902, a Wesley Deaconess Institute was founded in Ilkley to provide accommodation and training facilities for 27 students. By 1907, there were 98 fully trained deaconesses, 56 probationers and 19 accepted for training (Lloyd, 2010, p. 249). Bowman set down three principles which in time became a classic frame of reference for the Order (Graham, 2002, p. 241):

> There should be vocation but no vow...
> There should be discipline but not servility...
> There should be association but it should not exclude freedom...

Meanwhile other Methodist deaconess associations were coming into being. In 1887, Katherine Price Hughes, actively supported by her husband the Rev Hugh Price Hughes, set up the Sisters of the People based at the Wesleyan West London Mission. The association was neither subject to nor officially recognized by the Wesleyan Conference thus, unlike most sisterhoods, was relatively free from male control. This helped it to embrace an active stance towards women's rights (Lloyd, p. 251).

These initiatives encouraged the Rev Thomas John Cope of the United Methodist Free Churches based in Pimlico, London, in 1890 to set up a sisterhood on similar lines. A year later he founded a deaconess institute for these sisters. In 1907, this branch of Methodism amalgamated with the United Methodist Church and the sisters took the title of the United Methodist Deaconess Order (Graham, pp. 337-363).

In 1891, the Rev James Flannigan, a Primitive Methodist minister based in Southwark, inspired by the example of the West London Mission, began to recruit women for another association of deaconesses, also known as Sisters of the People.

These deaconess orders grew and flourished over subsequent decades. They all adopted a collective discipline and regarded themselves as religious communities. Their training was taken very seriously, at Ilkley deaconesses undergoing 'at least two years' of study and practical placements (Graham, p. 352). They worked long hours. Almost all were paid though they existed on a very small 'allowance'. Most deaconesses were between twenty-two and thirty five years of age (Lloyd, p. 252) and had to remain unmarried if they wished to remain in their associations.

Overall control of the different associations remained very largely in male hands.

The unification of Methodism and after

1932 saw the unification of Wesleyan Methodism, the United Methodist Church and Primitive Methodism. Within two years the deaconess associations of all these branches of Methodism came together under the title of the Wesley Deaconess Order. Overall this then had a membership of some 370 deaconesses (Graham, p 353). In 1936, the Methodist Book of Offices included a service of ordination for deaconesses who before that had been 'consecrated'. However, ordination was to a lay order and took place at Convocation not the Methodist Conference. The years following unification were not easy for the Order due to circuit re-organization and the economic depression. World War II saw deaconesses actively engaged in a very wide diversity of roles.

The post-war period brought a revolution in both state welfare provision and the role of women in society. These and other changes had a major impact on the Wesley Deaconess Order. From 1963 onwards deaconesses who married were permitted to remain in the Order. In the late 1960s the membership of the Order dropped to some 70 active deaconesses. This decline in strength led, in 1968, to Ilkley House being closed. Training was moved to Handsworth College in Birmingham and combined with that of presbyters. Three years later a new headquarters was opened near the college.

Another major change in the life of the Order occurred when Methodist presbyteral ministry was opened to women in 1973. Between 1973 and 1982, some 65 deaconesses were ordained as presbyters. It was suggested that a Methodist Order of Deacons be formed for those wishing to remain in the Order and that the latter be open to men. However, events overtook these proposals and, as a result of many deaconesses opting to become presbyters and a decline in numbers, the Methodist Conference decided that recruitment to the Order should cease from 1978.

Re-opening of the Methodist Diaconal Order

The years following the cessation of recruitment led to much heart-searching not least because of the valued legacy of the Wesley Deaconess

Order and an ongoing conviction that its life and work were in transition rather than facing termination. As a result, in 1986, the Methodist Conference agreed to re-open the Order to men as well as women. From that time onwards, the Order which had in the past had a good deal of financial, administrative and educational independence came more fully under the direction of the Methodist Conference. In 1988 the Order's name was changed to the Methodist Diaconal Order and, in 1990, the first ordinations to the new Order took place.

In 1993, the MDO was recognized by the Methodist Conference as an order of ministry and a religious order, thus bringing the designation of deacons as lay people to an end. However, it was not until 1998 that, by a standing vote, the Conference received all members of the Methodist Diaconal Order into 'Full Connexion', thus formally instituting the Methodist Diaconal Order as an order of ministry. The stipend of and accommodation for a deacon became the same as that required for a presbyter, a not unimportant development.

Since its re-opening in 1986, the Methodist Diaconal Order had been reflecting on its life as a religious order. Elements of this way of life, though differing from some of the hall-marks of the traditional religious orders, reach well back into the days of the Wesley Deaconess Order. In the early 1990s, a rule of life was drawn up by members of the Order and in 1993, as noted above, the Methodist Diaconal Order was affirmed as a religious order by the Methodist Conference.

The twenty-first century

In 2004, a report called *What is a Deacon?*, which set out a profile of the Order as an order of ministry and a religious order, was accepted by the Methodist Conference. Over the first decade of the twenty-first century the membership of the Methodist Diaconal Order steadily grew.

However, the contraction of the membership of the Methodist Church as a whole led to increasing financial constraints and, in 2014, the diaconal house in Edgbaston, Birmingham, was sold and the Order's headquarters moved to Methodist Church House in London. Meanwhile diaconal training, some of which had previously been dispersed across the country, was centred on the Queen's Foundation in Birmingham.

In 2018, there were 127 Methodist deacons in the active work, 9 student deacons and 118 supernumerary (retired) deacons. The MDO had 27 'Associates' of the Order and a number of 'Friends' who commit themselves to support the Order through prayer and advocacy.

Deacons are 'stationed' across the country. This means that the MDO is a widely dispersed community – from Shetland to the Channel Islands. However, this dispersal is balanced by deacons gathering annually at a three day Convocation, by the provision of area groups, and a range of networking facilities now much assisted by the Internet. Though being able to express a preference for the type of work they wish to do, deacons are 'stationed' by the Order for an average of about five years in places requesting their services. In recent years, the procedures for dealing with the selection, training and placement of deacons have become more closely integrated with those for presbyters.

Since its re-opening in 1986, the leadership of the MDO has experienced a number of changes in the form of its leadership. The Warden has become a deacon (previously a presbyter had occupied this role). Since 1986, all Wardens have been women, chosen by Convocation and approved by the Methodist Conference. A Deputy Warden (sometimes a man) has been in post for most of this period. For a few years in the first decade of the twenty-first century a 'voluntary' team ministry approach was attempted. In 2014, a Leadership Group, made up of lay people, presbyters and deacons, was appointed by the Methodist Conference to support the Warden and Deputy Warden and facilitate pastoral care for members of the Order.

Two other important Methodist reports

In 2016, the Methodist Conference received a report entitled the *Ministerial Code of Conduct*[1]. This document had been drawn up by a working party commissioned to draft a code of conduct for Methodist presbyters and deacons, identifying appropriate attitudes and behaviour by ministers in a wide range of situations and circumstances. A similar code had been produced for clergy in the Church of England. The Conference commended the draft code to the Methodist Church for

---

[1] www.methodist.org.uk/.../counc-mc17-18-ministerial-code-of-conduct-january-2017

consultation and comment. The report raises important questions about the calling and role of deacons and presbyters. It is the subject of Paper 2.

In 2018, the Faith and Order bodies of the Church of England and the Methodist Church presented a report to the General Synod and Methodist Conference entitled *Ministry and Mission in Covenant*[1]. This was the culmination of many conversations between the two churches over previous decades. Its main recommendation concerns how the interchangeability of the ministries of presbyters across both churches might be achieved. The process of achieving such interchangeability raises many issues which relate not only to the ethos and ecclesiology of Methodism, but to the place of a renewed diaconate within it. Paper 9 in this book is my response to this report.

Theological and ecclesiological foundations

No credible case can be made for envisioning the shape of the church to come, the form of its leadership and the calling of a renewed diaconate in relation to this, unless there is clarity about the theology and ecclesiology underpinning that vision. Nor can there be clarity about any theology and ecclesiology underpinning any future church unless there is also clarity about the context of its mission. I have explored the foundations of such a theology and ecclesiology elsewhere (Clark, 2005, 2008, 2016). However, I briefly describe these foundations here as the papers published in this book revisit them and build upon them.

My contention is that every theology and ecclesiology needs to reflect the social and political context of its day if the mission of the church is to be credible and purposeful. The context of our day is a world more wealthy and healthy than ever before, yet facing challenges more threatening to its future than humankind has ever encountered. These challenges not only relate to such formidable issues as climate change and the use of nuclear power. They are concerned, as the current political maelstrom shows all too clearly, with whether we can learn to live and work together as a global community of communities.

This fact brings an understanding of the nature of community to the very top of the agenda. It also raises the question of how we can

---

[1] www.churchofengland.org/sites/default/.../mission-and-ministry-in-covenant.pdf

get a handle on the deeper meaning of 'community', an often over-used and trivialised concept. I have explored at some depth the meaning of community from a sociological standpoint elsewhere (Clark, 2005). Building on that exploration, I believe that, in the image of the kingdom community, the Christian faith offers humankind a glimpse of both the meaning and power of community at its zenith. I argue that, theologically, the kingdom community's hall-marks are the gifts of life, liberation, love and learning. These communal gifts are of inestimable importance for the creation of one world and the flourishing of humankind.

What then of ecclesiology in relation to the shape of the church to come? If the gifts of the kingdom community are what humankind needs to claim and use if it is to survive and flourish, then the calling of the church is to become the servant of that community. That makes the church 'a diaconal', or servant, church. Its mission is to enable every human collective, from the family to the nation state and beyond, to become kingdom communities, and thereby to manifest the gifts of life, liberation love and learning in an inclusive and universal way.

The primary resource on which the diaconal church needs to draw to be able engage in this mission is its laity, the people of God in the world. The responsibility of its ordained leadership is to equip lay people for this task. A major concern of these papers is to argue that, within the diaconal church, the calling of a renewed diaconate is to enable the laity to engage in building kingdom communities wherever they live, work or play. I believe that such a diaconate is an inestimable gift of God to the present age. Within the diaconal church, and complementary to that gift, the calling of the presbyter is to ensure the creation and continuity of the gathered church as an exemplification of the kingdom community.

In these papers, I define the calling of a renewed diaconate as the deacon's sense of a divine imperative to enable the people of God to engage in ministry and the mission within society. When I speak of the role or responsibilities of a renewed diaconate, I mean the particular actions and attitudes needed, and the special skills and experience required by deacons to fulfil that calling. The same distinction between calling and role also relate to presbyteral ministry.

To be the servant of the kingdom community, the diaconal church needs to be empowered by a communal spirituality. Only in this way will the people of God be able to acquire those skills of discernment needed to identify where the gifts of the kingdom community are present or negated, and, in the light of that discernment, gain the experience and power to intervene.

If the church to come is to be a diaconal church, a very demanding journey lies ahead. This is because the church in the West is still shaped by the mould of Christendom. It is also because many forms of the so-called 'emerging church', be they in the West or in the numerically impressive church-going context of the South and East, are in danger of replicating communally inhibiting features of Christendom. These include theological fundamentalism, dominating forms of clericalism and a narrow sectarianism. Any genuine church of the future must possess a vision of what it means to be a diaconal church and be committed to making that vision a reality.

The papers

Much of the material in these papers echoes that published in my book *Building Kingdom Communities – with the diaconate as a new order of mission* (2016). It also reflects the content of my blog at www.diaconalchurch. com. However, these papers develop further many of the concepts and ideas covered in both, especially in relation to the future of British Methodism.

The papers themselves have been arranged by theme, rather than according to the order in which they were written. This is to aid awareness of the issues covered. However, because each paper was originally meant to be free-standing, there is some overlap in the material presented which I have not attempted to edit out. I hope such duplication will help to reinforce the points made rather than lessen the reader's attention.

Paper 1 explores further the foundational theology and ecclesiology briefly considered above, and which undergirds the material presented in all the other papers. The remaining papers focus on more specific issues. A preamble to each paper is intended to help readers to be aware of the context in which the paper was written, and the particular concerns it seeks to address. I believe that all the papers have vital implications not only for Methodism but for every church prepared to respond to God's gift of a renewed diaconate and of the diaconal church to come.

I make no claim that the papers present a final word on the issues considered. Their intention is to stimulate a debate which is currently in danger of lacking a radical vision for the future and which could potentially negate the gift of a renewed diaconate to church and world.

An Appendix explores the affinity between the concept of 'communal holiness', which I see as a core aspect of Methodist theology, and the concept of the kingdom community. The theses at the end of this book seek to summarise key features of a renewed diaconate and of the diaconal church.

The nine papers, taken together, form the main content of the book. They are preceded by an address delivered by the President of DIAKONIA, Sandy Boyce, at the World Diaconal Federation Assembly's meeting in Chicago in the summer of 2017, and attended by 400 representatives of diaconal associations worldwide. This address refers in a number of places to two of my earlier books (Clark, 2005 and 2016) and helps to set the scene for the papers following.

Visions for the future

Sandy Boyce

Preamble

This address was given by the President of DIAKONIA, the Rev (Deacon) Sandy Boyce, to the 22nd DIAKONIA World Federation Assembly of diaconal associations meeting in Chicago in July 2017. Sandy Boyce is a deacon at Pilgrim Uniting Church, a city congregation in the heart of Adelaide, and part of the Uniting Church in Australia. She was President of DIAKONIA from 2013, and was re-elected in 2017.

Her address reveals how the contribution of a renewed diaconate to the church to come – explored in my books *Breaking the Mould of Christendom* (2005) and *Building Kingdom Communities – with the diaconate as a new order of mission* (2016) – is currently being debated worldwide.

'Shaken by the Wind'

During my term as President of DIAKONIA World Federation, I have learned just how diverse are the expressions of diaconal ministry around the world and how diverse are the structures in which diaconal ministry is couched. There is no one way – but we have found we can all learn from each other. And that's the great work, I believe, of the DIAKONIA World Federation, that within and between the member associations we can all learn from the experience of the other, to affirm as well as to be a catalyst for change when need be.

It is worth briefly pausing to look at the development of the Deaconess movement in 1836 under the leadership of a German Lutheran pastor, Theodor Fliedner. It was a response to the challenging contextual issues of the day, especially with the rise of industrialisation, the movement from rural areas to the cities for employment, the subsequent rise of the urban poor who lacked the community support they might have enjoyed in rural communities, the rapid spread of disease, the end of the Napoleonic wars that left society in upheaval, and so on. It was into this particular context that Fliedner established a deaconess motherhouse and a diaconal community that would enable women in the 19th century to find a meaningful vocation and that would respond to these challenges in society.

Now, I want to suggest that this direct correlation between the context as the catalyst for the shape and ordering of ministry may at times be disconnected. It is necessary from time to time to step back from the immediacy of 'doing' ministry, to reflect on the pressing challenges for our time, and how may we together respond through releasing lay and ordained people to exercise ministry and mission within the church and in the community

You know the many current challenges in the world – globalisation, the unjust distribution of resources, weapons of mass destruction, the rise of terrorism, increasing disparity between the rich and the poor, complex inter-faith relations, accelerating climate change, the worldwide refugee crisis, to name but a few. The pressing overarching question may be, how can we live together in peace as a global community? The particular question for the church may be, how do we respond most effectively to this particular context in which we find ourselves?

Using the example of Theodor Fliedner and the development of the deaconess movement, the question may be: what kind of model for ministry is required in our time and place, for our particular context? (We have heard this morning some thoughtful insights about that.) David Clark in his two books, *Breaking the Mould of Christendom* and *Building Kingdom Communities*, offers very compelling arguments for a new way of thinking. He provides a comprehensive vision of church and ministry from a diaconal perspective. The movement is away from what is '*done to*' people, and towards collaborative and collective action – what people do *together* to address the issues and needs of the day.

It is a movement from diaconal ministry as something Deacons undertake on behalf of the church 'out there' to Deacons equipping and empowering the laity, the whole people of God, for diaconal ministry, and Deacons collaborating in collective action with others in the community, beyond the four walls of the church.

It places Deacons within the heart of the congregation – visioning, animating, equipping, empowering, sending. It places Deacons within the heart of the community – building relationships, standing in solidarity, drawing alongside people and groups, committing to collective and collaborative action in cooperation with community groups to work towards an outcome that enables flourishing for all.

'The role of Deacon is not so much a personal vocation lived out in the community, but a vocation that releases all members – the whole people of God – to live out their baptism in service in the community, to recognise, encourage, develop and release those gifts in God's people which will enable them to share in the ministry of caring, serving, healing, restoring, making peace and advocating justice as they go about their daily lives.' (*Report on Ministry in the Uniting Church 1991 Assembly*)

The role of the diaconate is very much a live issue for Deacons in the Methodist Church in the UK, where there is currently a debate about the future of the Methodist Diaconal Order. David Clark suggests that the kind of leadership required for a church that orients its life towards diaconal ministry requires new understandings about leadership. He suggests that Presbyters (Leaders and Pastors and Ministers) take responsibility for the renewal of the gathered church through accessing the kingdom community's gifts of life, liberation, love and learning.

The diaconate as an order of mission would assume responsibility for furthering the ministry of the laity as the church dispersed in the world, educating and equipping lay people for their task of building communities which make manifest the gifts of the kingdom community throughout the whole of society.

David Bosch's definition of mission picks up this idea of 'participation in the liberating mission of Jesus, the good news of God's love incarnated in the witness of a community for the sake of the world'.

What flexibility do we need in how we are church together in order to respond to the particular context and challenges of our time? What ways of organizing ourselves as church will best enable a collective response to a particular context – social, political, economic?

Inga Bengtzon served 65 years as a Deaconess, and served for 13 years as the President of DIAKONIA World Federation. She was a visionary. Referring to the General Assembly of the WCC in 1983, she argued for the inclusion of a self-critical dimension of the diaconal role that challenges the church's 'locked, frozen, static and self-centred structures' in order to turn them into a 'workable, living instrument for the church's task of healing, reconstruction and sharing with each other.' *Diakonia*, she said, cannot be limited to institutional forms. It must 'break through the already established structures and demarcations in the institutional church' in order to act, heal, and build in the world. (*Bengtzon, 1984,* translated from Swedish).

David Clark casts his vision to what he calls the kingdom community and suggests that in order to be able to undertake a kingdom-focused mission, the church has first of all to break the mould of Christendom, and become a diaconal or servant church, where all the ministries serve that purpose, and all the ministries orient themselves to servant leadership. The diaconate should be responsible for encouraging and equipping the laity to exercise their ministry of kingdom community building in every sphere of the life of society. What will enable us to most fully respond to God's mission in and through the church? It's a question for us all, and particularly how we orient what we name as church to be a kingdom community with a kingdom-focused mission.

And I return to the question I asked when I introduced Theodor Fliedner's initiative to establish a deaconess community in 1836 in Germany: what kind of model for ministry is required in our time and place, for our particular context? How can the church best shape ministry so that the diaconal mission of the whole people of God can be best equipped?

It is a continuing conversation and perhaps calls for a conversion of how we 'do' church.

1

Kingdom community, diaconal church and the liberation of the laity

Preamble

In 2013, the Methodist Council requested the Methodist Conference of that year to direct Methodism's Faith and Order Committee 'in consultation with the Methodist Diaconal Order, to undertake work on the theology and ecclesiology underpinning the diaconate in Methodism, its place within the British Connexion and its place within the universal church' (Methodist Council Paper, 2013). This request stemmed from some uncertainty as to the place of the Warden of the Methodist Diaconal Order (MDO) within the leadership of the Connexion. However, the working party considering that matter discerned that a much fuller appraisal of the place of the diaconate, and implicitly other ministries within Methodism and beyond, needed to be undertaken for the benefit of the Connexion as a whole. The Methodist Council and Conference agreed.

Consequently a working party of the Faith and Order Committee was set up to address this brief.[1] Its Interim Report was submitted to and approved by the Methodist Conference in July 2016. However, in its final paragraph the report states (6.7):

> It is further recognised that many of these questions (regarding the Methodist Diaconal Order) relate to our understanding of ministry and oversight and they cannot therefore be explored in isolation. The Faith and Order Committee therefore presents this interim report to the Conference, with the intention of bringing a final response (concerning the MDO) *as part of the work on ministry in the Methodist Church* [my italics] to the 2018 Conference.

---

[1] In transmission, the original brief given by the Methodist Conference somehow lost the broader and very important ecumenical context originally intended. Thus the Interim Report (2016) of this working party simply describes its brief as an exploration of 'The Theology and Ecclesiology Underpinning the Diaconate'.

In fact, the 'final' report to the Methodist Conference on the Methodist Diaconal Order has been postponed until 2019. An interim report on *Ministry in the Methodist Church* as a whole was brought to the Conference of 2018, with a final report scheduled for 2020. Thus explorations of diaconal and presbyteral orders within the Methodist Church would appear to be running in parallel. Whether this will help or hinder the emergence of new insights into the nature of a renewed diaconate and the relationship between the two orders remains to be seen.

In Paper 1 is set out the theology and ecclesiology which I believe needs to be the foundation of the church to come, what I call 'the diaconal church', and of a renewed diaconate as a hall-mark of leadership within the latter. I also explore the potential contribution of the Methodist Church, and especially of its diaconal and presbyteral ministries, to such a church.

1 Introduction

My own ministry as both a presbyter and a deacon, and many years of reflection on how these two ministries might complement each other, leads me to believe that the exploration of 'ministry in the Methodist Church' now underway is potentially of great importance. This is because it has significant implications not only for diaconal, presbyteral and lay ministries as such, but for the mission of British Methodism *and* the wider church.

However, I believe that the exploration underway needs to engage in a radical re-appraisal of the theology and ecclesiology underpinning not only the diaconate but the ministries of the whole of Methodism. This could open the way for Methodism to reclaim its distinctive heritage as a holiness movement [see Appendix], as urged by the President at the Methodist Conference in July 2016, and check Methodism's drift towards becoming an institution which all too often clones the theology and ecclesiology of other more historically established denominations. It would also enable Methodism to make a distinctive and much needed contribution to the ecumenical movement, at present at a somewhat low-ebb within the UK. Above all, it would inspire Christians to engage more energetically and effectively with the critical issues facing our society and world at a time of profound political and cultural change.

I offer this paper as a personal contribution to the current debate. I do so as one who has been immensely grateful for what Methodism has offered me and concerned that what it stands for is not lost to posterity.

This paper deliberately broadens the focus of the ongoing exploration from the life and work of Methodist Diaconal Order to the future of all Methodist ministries, diaconal, presbyteral *and* lay. However, the paper is also relevant to the important discussions taking place within all denominations concerning the divine gift of 'a renewed diaconate' and the contribution it needs to be making to the world church.[1] Consequently, I believe that much of what I set out below is not only applicable to the Methodist Diaconal Order but to all diaconal orders, and not only of relevance to the relationship between Methodist orders of ministry, but to that relationship within every denomination.

---

[1] See, for example, the discussions taking place in many other churches:

Anglican-Lutheran

The Diaconate as an Ecumenical Opportunity. The Hanover Report (1996). Report of the Anglican-Lutheran International Commission

To Love and Serve the Lord – Diakonia in the Life of the Church. The Jerusalem Report (2012).

Report of the Anglican-Lutheran International Commission (ALIC III)

Roman Catholicism

From the Diakonia of Christ to the Diakonia of the Apostles (2003). International Theological Commission. London: Catholic Truth Society

William T. Ditewig (2007) *The Emerging Diaconate – Servants Leaders in a Servant Church*. New York/Mahwah, NJ: Paulist Press

Church of England

For such a time as this. A renewed diaconate in the Church of England (2001). London: Church House Publishing

The Distinctive Diaconate (2003). Diocese of Salisbury

The Mission and Ministry of the Whole Church – Biblical, theological and contemporary perspectives (2007) The Faith and Order Advisory Group of the Church of England

Church of Scotland

Deacons of the Gospel – A Vision for Today : A Ministry for Tomorrow (2000) Church of Scotland

Deacons of Word and Service – the vision statement of the Church of Scotland diaconate (2018)

Episcopal Church in North America

Susanne Watson Epting (2015) *Unexpected Consequences – The Diaconate Renewed*. New York: Morehouse Publishing

The Iona Report – The Diaconate in the Anglican Church of Canada (2016) The General Synod of the Anglican Church of Canada

The discussion which follows is set within the context of a missional imperative, founded on a kingdom theology and diaconal ecclesiology. I am convinced that such a theology and ecclesiology must inform and empower the church to come if it is to make its unique and vital contribution to the flourishing of society and world.

2 A kingdom theology imperative for mission in today's world

2.1 The contemporary context of mission

Before we can say anything meaningful about the theology and ecclesiology underpinning the ministries of any church (including Methodism), it is imperative to get real about the rapidly changing context of mission.

One of the most influential features of contemporary life is that human beings have become more mobile than ever before. Humanity has become geographically mobile (not only individuals but whole populations are now on the move), economically mobile (the globalization of the market), cognitively mobile (the Internet and, not least, social media, increasingly eliminate time and space as barriers to communication), socially mobile (the massive developments in education, especially literacy and numeracy, are breaking down traditional hierarchies) and culturally mobile (there is a universal emergence of 'rainbow nations'). Mobility on this massive scale has a number of consequences. On the one hand, it liberates billions of people to enjoy unprecedented freedom of movement and life-style choices (including who or what they worship). On the other hand, it breaks down the bonds of family, locality and nation threatening the security and identity of those who seek to hang on to a more settled and predictable way of life.

To make the future even more challenging, mass mobility has been accompanied by a number of immensely destabilising factors, including the development of weapons of mass destruction, a global population explosion, accelerating climate change and a worldwide refugee crisis.

These issues mean that humankind is facing accelerating and disturbing change on a scale hitherto never experienced before. Nevertheless, behind these 'presenting' issues lies an even deeper crisis – a worldwide weakening of communal bonds and the fear of the loss of identity that goes with it. Consequently, because humanity has to find its way to becoming a global community of communities if it is to survive and flourish, it is imperative that the quest for community moves to the very top of the agenda. However, that quest must be for a form of community which is open and inclusive, not xenophobic and exclusive. In this context, the experience of Brexit, the dilemmas facing the European Community, the Trump phenomenon and the fragmentation of the Middle East are simply indicators of the challenges ahead.

2.2 A communal focus for a contemporary theology of mission

It should be abundantly clear, therefore, that the mission of the church in our day and age must be, first and foremost, concerned with the future of humankind and not the survival of the church. The gospel for our time is a vision of community at its zenith, the kingdom community, and the offer of the power to make that vision a reality

The gospel of the kingdom community, as I interpret it, is founded on the nature of the divine community, the Trinity and its transformational gifts. Elsewhere (Clark, 2005), I have suggested that these gifts embrace sociological hall-marks of community. However, theologically, they can be identified as 4Ls – the gift of life offered by God the Creator; the gift of liberation, offered by Christ the Liberator; the gift of love, offered by the Holy Spirit the Unifier; and the gift of learning, offered by the Trinity as a learning community (Clark, 2016, pp. 12-18). It is these gifts that Christ associated with the essence of the kingdom, taught about throughout his ministry, exemplified in his life and death and which he entrusted to his followers to offer to others.

I believe that the mission of the church is to discern where the gifts of the kingdom community are already manifest within society and world, and to intervene to enable them to be given the fullest possible expression. Where these gifts are neglected or rejected, the church's mission is to challenge the status quo, and seek to do all in its power to bring these gifts to the fore.[1] However, such a mission can be a very costly undertaking, as the cross demonstrates only too well.

---

[1] See for example, *Reclaiming Jesus – a confession of faith in a time of crisis* (Easter, 2018). A declaration by church leaders in the USA. Download from www.reclaimingjesus.org

At the same time, if the church is to engage with any credibility and effectiveness in its kingdom community building mission, the medium has to be the message. For this to happen, the mould of Christendom, that institutional form which has shaped the life and work of the church for too long, has to be broken.

3 A diaconal ecclesiology imperative for mission in today's world

3.1 A diaconal ecclesiology

The theology of a kingdom community building mission sketched out above has profound implications for the ecclesiology of the church and its leadership. Below, I summarise what I see as the most significant of these implications.

o The Christendom church must give way to the diaconal church (see *The Jerusalem Report,* 2012).
o The diaconal church is the servant of the kingdom community.
o Its mission is making manifest the gifts of the kingdom community – life, liberation, love and learning – throughout society and world.
o The diaconal church liberates and equips the laity, the church's primary missionary resource, to discern and make manifest the gifts of the kingdom community within every sphere of life – from the family to education, health and welfare to leisure, business to commerce, law and order to government. Thus the mission of the laity is to be kingdom community builders.
o To facilitate its mission the diaconal church requires new forms of leadership.

3.2 Leadership within the diaconal church

The leadership of the diaconal church is founded on an ecclesiology which upholds the principle that 'no priesthood exists which belongs exclusively to a particular order or class' (*Methodist Deed of Union*, 1932, Section 2, Clause 4). To engage in kingdom community building within society and world, the diaconal church requires new forms of leadership based on a clear and distinctive division of labour. I suggest that these should be:

A renewed presbyteral ministry **taking the form of**
   '*an order of continuity***' –**
   assuming responsibility for deepening the life and work of
   the gathered church by nourishing the gifts of the kingdom
   community within it.

A renewed diaconate **taking the form of** *'an order of mission'* **–**
   assuming responsibility for equipping the laity to build
   communities which manifest the gifts of the kingdom
   community within every sector of society. A renewed
   diaconate, already up and coming, is a unique gift to the
   church worldwide.

4 How Methodism currently manifests the signs of a diaconal church

Few churches as yet manifest many hall-marks of the diaconal church
and the new forms of leadership needed for it to fulfil its mission.
However, my conviction is that Methodism comes as close as most
in reflecting the missional and ecclesiological vision of a diaconal
church.

I note below some important diaconal hall-marks present within the
life and work of the Methodist Church today.

   o Methodism retains many features of its origins as a holiness
     movement, a concept which, as I argue elsewhere embraces
     the gifts of the kingdom community [see Appendix].
   o Within Methodism, lay people are seen as the church's
     primary mission resource.
   o As stated in its *Deed of Union*, the Methodist Church mirrors
     the diaconal church in that the ministries of laity, presbyter
     and deacon are held to be of equal standing.
   o Methodism is a profoundly communal church with a strong
     emphasis on 'fellowship' and pastoral care.
   o Methodism's character as a mutually supportive 'Connexion'
     reflects an important communal hall-mark of the diaconal
     church.
   o Methodism has always had a deep concern for the poor and
     marginalized as an essential focus of mission.

o The Methodist Church has consistently been in the van of the ecumenical movement in Britain, mirroring the diaconal church's commitment to inclusivity and universality.

Nevertheless, British Methodism has not always appreciated the importance of the deeply communal nature of its theology and the diaconal character of its ecclesiology. Thus it remains in danger of neglecting or losing that which can offer a great deal to the diaconal church to come. Nor has it always grasped the significance of the life and work of the MDO as God's gift of a renewed diaconate. This gift offers the means of developing further the most creative aspects of Methodism's theology and ecclesiology, of reshaping its approach to mission and of bringing into being new forms of leadership.

5 The implications for the Methodist Diaconal Order of embracing a kingdom theology and diaconal ecclesiology

5.1 Signs of the kingdom community in practice

At the heart of the missional theology, which should inspire Christians engaged in a world facing communal fragmentation, are the gifts of the kingdom community – life, liberation, love and learning – and the power of these gifts to transform chaos into community. For the church, including Methodism, the call to build a world transformed by those gifts is, I believe, a divine imperative at the heart of mission. So how can Methodists discern those signs of the kingdom community which might offer guidance in building kingdom communities here and now?

Many such signs exist in world and church. However, we are often blind to them because they frequently appear in the commonplace happenings of daily life and work[1]. Whenever and wherever we do discern them, they need to be recognised as gifts of grace and treated as extremely precious. For me, the life of the MDO, with all its inevitable human limitations, offers Methodism and the wider church many insights into what mission as kingdom community building might mean. In this context, it is interesting that Anthony Reddie has described the Methodist Diaconal Order as 'Methodism's best kept secret' and

---

[1] For examples of such glimpses within the world of work see Clark (2014).

Helen Cameron as 'yeast in the dough of Methodism' (*Who do you say we are?* paras. 6 and 15).

5.2 Implications of embracing a kingdom theology and diaconal ecclesiology for the Methodist Diaconal Order as *a religious order*

My experience of ten years in the Order is that deacons know 'in their guts' that their life as a religious community powerfully bonds, supports and inspires them as an Order. However, I believe that Methodism has yet to appreciate fully why the MDO's work as an order of ministry *and* (the word *'and'* is all-important) a religious order need to remain 'completely intertwined' (*What is a Deacon?* para. 3.5).

Such 'intertwining' is essential not least because, if the building of kingdom communities is to take pride of place in mission, it is the life of the MDO *as a religious community* which offers a model, to church and world, of what collectives transformed by the gifts of the kingdom community might look like. The medium (the MDO as a religious community) must exemplify the message (the need for all collectives, sacred and secular, to become kingdom communities).

The important insights into the nature of the kingdom community offered by the MDO as a religious order are not so much about its forms and structures. They are about how the Order exemplifies the kingdom community's gifts of life, liberation, love and learning. I have described in some detail elsewhere ways in which I see the MDO, *as a religious order*, offering Methodism, the wider church and, indeed, world, invaluable insights into what the gifts of the kingdom community might look like in practice (Clark, 2013). This is why the MDO can be designated 'a tool of Christian mission' (Interim Report, 5.3.7). It is also one response to the Interim Report's questioning as to what Methodism and the wider church have to learn from the MDO (Interim Report, 5.1; 5.2; 6.1; 6.4).

5.3 Implications of embracing a kingdom theology and diaconal ecclesiology for the Methodist Diaconal Order as *an order of ministry*

The MDO needs to derive a deeper understanding of its mission from the way in which its life *as a religious order* manifests the kingdom community's gifts of life, liberation, love and learning. However, this distinctive missional contribution to Methodism and the wider church

25

could be further enhanced if, whilst retaining its designation as an order of ministry, the MDO built on the attributes of the latter to help it develop into *an order of mission*. What would be some key features of the MDO becoming an order of mission?

o The apostolate of an order of mission would be, first and foremost, concerned with the communal transformation of society, not the maintenance of the gathered church.

o As an order of mission, the MDO's primary task would be to further kingdom community building across all sectors of daily life – in schools, hospitals, shops and offices, businesses, centres of government and situations wherever people live, work and play.

o The heart of such an apostolate would be enabling, educating and equipping the people of God – the church's primary mission resource – to become kingdom community builders alongside those of other faiths or none. This will entail liberating the laity from over-dependency on the ordained ministry.

o As members of an order of mission, the primary calling of the diaconate would be to assume the role and responsibilities of *mission enablers*.

A renewed diaconate would thus be acknowledging that the calling of the permanent diaconate has always been profoundly contextual. Thus, in the West at least, there is now an urgent need to move away from the assumption that the primary calling of the deacon is that of 'witness through service' and, more recently, 'jack-of-all-trades'. Instead, the deacon's calling as mission enabler needs to come to the fore – embodying the sense of a divine imperative to educate and equip the people of God to engage in the building of kingdom communities within every sector of society.

It is interesting to note here that a frequently used 'mission statement' of the MDO feels after, even if the Order does not as yet fully embrace, this shift of priorities. It states that the MDO is 'a mission focused, pioneering religious community committed to *enabling* (my italics) outreach, evangelism and service in God's world'. Such a statement points forward towards the primary calling of Methodist deacons becoming that of 'mission *enablers*' of the people of God dispersed in the world.

o It is recognized that at certain times an order of mission will need to encourage the initiatives of diaconal pioneers. However, the primary calling of the deacon to be a mission enabler means a commitment to encourage and equip others to take responsibility for any such diaconal initiative taken as soon as is feasible.

6 The implications for Methodist presbyters of embracing a kingdom theology and diaconal ecclesiology

[The issues discussed in this section are developed more fully in Paper 8]

6.1 Implications of embracing a kingdom theology and diaconal ecclesiology for presbyters *as an order of ministry*

Within the diaconal church, alongside deacons developing as an order of mission, presbyters need to become *an order of continuity*. This means their drawing on the enduring riches of the church, bequeathed by Christendom at its best, in order to create the gathered church as another model of the kingdom community (alongside that of the MDO as a religious order). In this capacity, presbyters would have the explicit responsibility of enabling the gathered church, be it inherited, planted or 'a fresh expression', to manifest the gifts of the kingdom community – life, liberation, love and learning.

Within the diaconal church, many gathered churches will need to refocus their life and work to fulfil their calling as servants of the kingdom community. For unless the gifts of the latter are clearly evident in and through the life of the gathered church, kingdom community building within society and world becomes an impossible task. In short, the medium of the gathered church must embody its message.

To describe presbyters as 'an order of continuity' in no way devalues their calling as an order of ministry. Continuity is quite different from 'maintenance'. A ministry of continuity requires presbyters not only to tap into the rich resources of the past but to develop them for the future. It involves presbyters enabling members of the gathered church, through worship, education in the faith and pastoral care, to gain the inspiration, resources and resilience to engage in kingdom community building in daily life.

Within the diaconal church, the presbyter is also engaged in mission. For example, presbyters will still be actively involved in *church* planting and developing fresh expressions of *church*. Nevertheless, the presbyter's primary concern will remain the communal development and enrichment of the life and work of the gathered church, inherited or newly established, rather than, as in the case of a renewed diaconate, educating and supporting the laity for their daily task of kingdom community building in the wider world.

6.2 Implications of embracing a kingdom theology and diaconal ecclesiology for presbyters *as a religious order*

Being a religious order enables deacons to empower and give direction to their apostolate as an order of mission enablers. Likewise, I believe that, in order to empower *and* give direction to their calling as an order of continuity, presbyters too should eventually become *a religious order* in their own right. This would help Methodism break the deadening grip of institutionalism and reclaim its heritage as a holiness *movement* [see Appendix].

6.3 The need for deacons and presbyters to be members of different religious orders

None the less, an important proviso needs to be added. Presbyters *as a religious order* should remain distinct from deacons as a religious order. Just as within the Roman Catholic and Anglican Churches, different apostolates have led to the emergence of different religious orders, so should be the case with Methodist deacons and presbyters. To amalgamate Methodist deacons and presbyters into a single religious order would confuse identities, undermine a sense of solidarity and weaken the distinctive apostolates of both.

7 Ensuring the equal standing of diaconal and presbyteral orders

The Methodist *Deed of Union* (1932, Section 2, Clause 4) states that: 'The Methodist Church holds the doctrine of the priesthood of all believers and consequently believes that no priesthood exists which belongs exclusively to a particular order or class of persons...'. Methodism is committed to a theology which espouses the equality of the ministries of presbyters, deacons and lay people. It is a principle which stands at the heart of Methodism as a 'Connexional' Church.

According to its theology of ministry, therefore, Methodism regards deacons and presbyters as orders of equal standing. Both are selected and trained in similar ways. Both are ordained at Conference and brought into 'full Connexion'. Both are on the same stipend and experience the same housing arrangements. However, in practice, most Methodists continue to regard the ministry of deacons as secondary to and, in many respects, dependent on that of presbyters. Here, Methodism is coming dangerously close to embracing the ecclesiology of those churches which uphold a hierarchical three-fold form of ministry, and to denying the profoundly important stance of its own *Deed of Union*. Consequently Methodism needs to address the kinds of issues mentioned below which perpetuate this ecclesiological anomaly.

7.1 Within the gathered church

I believe that deacons should *in principle* be authorized to preside at holy communion. For deacons *in principle* to be authorized to preside at holy communion does not mean that *in practice* this would happen frequently. However, if the MDO is to become an order of mission in genuine partnership with presbyters as an order of continuity, then deacons should be authorized to preside at holy communion as and when their responsibility for equipping the laity for their task of kingdom community building in the world makes this appropriate. This would also enable deacons to be able to administer holy communion beyond the walls of the church when needed to support lay people in their engagement with secular society.

Another significant development in enhancing the role of deacons in worship might be that they are authorized from time to time to preside over the washing of feet as a sacrament gaining increasing attention ecumenically and of particular relevance to the ministry of the people of God in the world. (Clark, 2016, pp. 151-152; O'Loughlin)

Overall, however, the diaconate, as an order of mission, needs to have a more distinctive and active role in worship, as is already beginning to happen in the Anglican and Roman Catholic Churches. In Methodism, this could include offering an exposition of 'the Word' (not necessarily as formally designated 'local preachers') and leading prayers to help affirm and encourage the kingdom community building mission of members of the congregation in daily life.

7.2 Across the Connexion

I believe two other developments are essential if the ministries of deacon and presbyter are to achieve parity of standing within the Connexion.

- o The presidency of the Methodist Conference, as well as the office of Chair of District, should be open to deacons. The current anomaly stems in part from deacons not being authorized to preside at holy communion. However, the Methodist Diaconal Order will never be able to make its distinctive contribution to reshaping the mission of Methodism if deacons are barred from the opportunity to lead the Connexion in the same way as presbyters.
- o The opportunity for presbyters to become members of the MDO should become as normative as the opportunity for deacons to become presbyters. In fact, both changes of ministerial identity are already permitted by the constitutional practice of the Methodist Church.

Up to the present time, only one Methodist presbyter has become a deacon (in stark contrast to a considerable number of deacons becoming presbyters). This 'one way traffic' may well be influenced by the fact that presbyters are unprepared to surrender their calling to preside at holy communion (Clark, 2016, pp. 189-90, 195-6).[1] However, it is a situation

---

[1] In 2005, when I moved from presbyteral to diaconal ministry, I was 'relieved' of my presbyteral commission to preside at holy communion, a commission which I had held for forty years as a Methodist presbyter. No one within Methodism appeared to give any thought as to the theological justification for this 'de-commissioning'.

which reveals Methodism's gradual drift away from the theology its own *Deed of Union* towards a hierarchical understanding of ordination

8 Changes required in selection, training, ordination and collective learning needed to further the ministry of deacons as an order of mission and presbyters as an order of continuity

8.1 Changes required to develop the ministry of deacons as an order of mission:

- o in *the selection process*
  - ensure that candidates are committed to becoming both members of an order of mission *and* of a religious order.
- o in *training* (pre- and post-ordination)
  - end diaconal training as a 'bolt-on' to presbyteral training and give it the time and attention it warrants.
  - enable those in training to understand and appreciate the theology and ecclesiology underpinning the diaconate as both an order of mission and a religious order.
  - offer deacons the professional skills required to fulfil the responsibilities of being members of an order of mission.
  - help deacons to become more aware of and confident in exercising their calling as servant leaders of the people of God in the world.
- o in *the ordination service*
  - include a commitment to the diaconate as a religious order.
- o in the *life of the Order*
  - develop more fully the Order's life as a learning community, notably through diaconal area groups and Convocation.

8.2 Changes needed to develop the ministry of presbyters as an order of continuity

These steps would be similar to those for deacons outlined above, only focusing on the theology and ecclesiology underpinning, and implications for *presbyters becoming an order of continuity and a religious order*.

9 Issues regarding numbers, spread and finance

9.1 Increasing the spread of and numbers within a diaconal order of mission

For the mission of Methodism as a diaconal church to be reshaped, at least one deacon should be stationed in every large circuit. Though the MDO has expanded in recent years, this raises the practical problem of there not being enough deacons to meet such a development.

However, I believe there are many people, lay and ordained, already employed by Methodism who are striving hard, in a pragmatic and often isolated way, to undertake the role of 'mission enablers'. Such people, and Methodism as a whole, would benefit immensely if they were offered the communal support, and a deeper understanding of the theology and ecclesiology underpinning their role, which would result from their becoming members of the MDO. Amongst those whom I include as potential members of an expanded diaconal order of mission are:

o those who currently assume the title of 'mission enabler'
o those designated as a 'learning and development officer' or with a similar title
o presbyters dedicated to working 'on the margins' of church and society
o chaplains who see their work as primarily missional rather than pastoral
o those training to form the new category of 'pioneer ministers'.
o lay people already building bridges between church and world in a voluntary capacity.

To those serving as 'mission enablers' whose circumstances prevent them becoming members of a renewed diaconal order, encouragement should be given to consider becoming members of a lay third order (see section 11 below).

Methodism also needs to address the realities of life and work in this day and age and develop a 'self-supporting' form of diaconal (as well as presbyteral[1]) ministry. A self-supporting diaconate is in fact the norm in many churches across the world.

It is worth noting here that an increase in the number of men, and of those from a variety of ethnic backgrounds, would be a welcome development for the MDO.

9.2 Financial requirements

Movement into the MDO as an order of mission of the kind of personnel noted above could be undertaken with relatively limited financial cost. Other funding might come from the following.

o Some large circuits in being, or coming into being, have funds which could be used to employ a deacon as a mission enabler.
o There may be Christian voluntary organizations operating within society (for example, Action for Children and MHA) willing to fund a deacon as a mission enabler related to their particular sphere of work.
o There might be trusts willing to fund a deacon to work at community building in relation to the development of secular (or religious) organizations.
o It is not out of the question that the 'launch' of a new order of mission within Methodism might attract additional giving from the Methodist people.
o Some funding from the sale of Methodism's redundant churches could go to support a new order.
o As already noted, the development of self-supporting ministries could help considerably here.

10 Changes in leadership, organization and accountability needed for the Methodist Diaconal Order to develop as an order of mission

10.1 Leadership issues

If the MDO grew in size and spread, there would need to be at least two Deputy Wardens, based in appropriate geographical locations, to serve

---

[1] It is of interest to note that, in 2016, there were 7788 stipendiary priests (declining) and 3230 self-supporting priests (increasing) in the Church of England. *Church Times* 7/9/2018, p.22

it. There would also need to be additional administrative support for the Warden and Deputy Wardens. A much closer bond would need to be forged between the MDO and District Chairs.

There is no reason to think that the responsibilities of the MDO's current Leadership Group, in relation to the support and accountability of the Warden and Deputy Warden(s), would need to change a great deal.

10.2 Changes in diaconal gatherings outside Convocation

To assist with bonding, oversight and administration, it would be valuable for an expanded Order to hold an annual regional 'convocation', sometime between annual national Convocations, for deacons serving in the south or the north of the country. Such regional gatherings have happened in the past.

In an expanded Methodist Diaconal Order, the function and agenda of area groups would be even more important than at present. Thus groups might need to take on a more structured form with area group leaders, though being nominated by area groups, appointed at and answerable to Convocation. Area groups might also be given more structured training responsibilities to help their members develop their skills as mission enablers.

11 Engaging lay people in actively supporting new diaconal and presbyteral orders

It would be immensely supportive for the new orders of deacons and presbyters if Methodism were to initiate the formation of two 'third orders', consisting largely but not exclusively of lay people. These would be similar to those associated with the historic religious orders, such as the Franciscans. One third order would be associated with the MDO as an order of mission; the other with presbyters as an order of continuity. Each third order would be seen as an integral part of the life and work of the diaconal order of mission and presbyteral order of continuity respectively, though less formally and fully involved than their ordained members. [For a full discussion of a diaconal lay 'third order' see Paper 7]

12 Ecumenical issues

12.1 What Methodism and the MDO could learn from other churches and Christian communities

Many denominations on the European and North American scenes have in recent years published reports of consultations on a permanent and/or a renewed diaconate (see Introduction footnote). These strongly affirm the significance of the permanent or distinctive diaconate for the renewal of the life and work of the church. However, despite helpful historical reviews of the ministry exercised by deacons in the past, few reports appear to grasp the importance of a renewed diaconate as *an order of mission*. Nor are many reports able to envisage breaking the mould of Christendom and the emergence of a renewed diaconate having genuine equality of standing with presbyters.

12.2 Learning from other forms of community, lay and religious

A good deal about the way in which having a rule of life can underpin and inform the apostolate of Christian groups and networks can be gained from what has been called 'the Christian Community Movement' (Clark, 1977; 1984; 2005, pp. 150-169) active over the last few decades of the twentieth century, as well as from the much smaller number of similar initiatives which have commenced since then [see Paper 6 on the new monasticism]. Typical communities which have much to offer are the Mennonites, Iona, Movement for a Better World, Taizé, Corrymeela and l'Arche. A number of older religious orders, such as the Franciscans, Little Sisters of Jesus, Sisters of Notre Dame, and certain lay Roman Catholic apostolates, also offer important guidelines for the future of Methodist orders.

12.3 What the development of a presbyteral order of continuity and a diaconal order of mission could offer other churches

British Methodism's contribution to the sustainability of the gathered (or parish) church is to work with the Church of England, the Anglican Church in Wales and the Church of Scotland north of the border, to explore how the combined resources of all denominations, including that of presbyters as an order of continuity, can be most effectively deployed.

Nevertheless, as an order of ministry and a religious order, the Methodist Diaconal Order is *already* blazing a trail concerning the potential of a renewed diaconate. For example, members of DACE (the Diaconal Association of the Church of England though sadly now disbanded) have on numerous occasions expressed their 'envy' of this feature of the Methodist diaconate.

At the same time, there is considerable interest within the United Methodist Church in the USA relating to the way in which the diaconal order has developed within British Methodism. And, as the Chicago Assembly address by the President of DIAKONIA in 2017 shows (see the first article in this book), some within the worldwide association of deacons are showing a keen interest in the idea that the permanent diaconate should now develop into an order of mission.

March 2017

2 The definition of the ministries of presbyter and deacon in Methodism's 'Ministerial Code of Conduct'

Preamble

In 2016, the Methodist Conference received a draft report entitled the *Ministerial Code of Conduct*[1]. This document had been drawn up by a working party commissioned to create a code of conduct for Methodist presbyters and deacons identifying appropriate attitudes and behaviour by ministers in a wide range of situations and circumstances. A similar code had been produced for clergy in the Church of England. The Conference commended the draft code to the Methodist Church for consultation and comment. Amongst the 'fundamental' principals adopted by the working party were:

o That the code should have an aspirational tone (i.e. it should offer a call to excellence in ministerial practice and behaviour), but also provide a set of tools with which (in)appropriate conduct and (in)competence can be identified and assessed.

o That the code is for ordained ministers; and that the shared nature of ministry is best expressed by there being a single code with occasional notes to clarify any differences in expectations for deacons/presbyters.

The intended 'aspirational tone' of the report means that it attempts to look to the future. This increases its significance, as how presbyteral and diaconal ministries are defined will have important implications for some time ahead. The fact that the code starts from the assumption that much of what it contains refers to both presbyters and deacons is encouraging in terms of what unites these ministries. However, this makes it all the more important to look carefully as to how the two forms of ministry are distinguished.

This paper argues that the definitions of 'presbyter' and 'deacon' employed in the code look backwards not forwards and fail to be

---

[1] www.methodist.org.uk/.../counc-mc17-18-ministerial-code-of-conduct-january-2017

'aspirational'. In reality, as these definitions stand, they are anachronistic. Consequently, they undermine an equality of leadership which should characterise the two orders concerned. The paper contends that the code reveals the urgent need for a re-appraisal of the future role and complementarity of presbyteral and diaconal ministries, not least to help reshape the mission of Methodism and to identify its special place within the universal church.

1 Definitions

1.1 Definitions of presbyteral and diaconal ministries

In the *Ministerial Code of Conduct,* the ministries of presbyters and deacons are defined in similar terms in two places [Vocation (ministry in the MCB) – column 2, and Leadership and collaboration – column 1]

The definitions of role, as quoted in the code under 'Leadership and collaboration', are as follows:

'Presbyters are called to a "principal and directing part" in [the] great duties [of the Church]'.
Deacons are called to "represent the servanthood of Christ, exercising a formal role of leadership in the Church".

The *Code of Conduct* draws the presbyteral definition from the 1932 Methodist Deed of Union (Section 2, Clause 4) and the diaconal definition from *What is a Deacon?* (2004, para. 7.3).

1.2. Contention of this paper

It is my contention that, accurate as these definitions are in relation to the faith and practice of the Methodist Church in the past, they are now outmoded and need re-appraisal. In particular, they fail to take on board the acceptance by the Methodist Conference, in 1993, of the Methodist Diaconal Order as an order of ministry *of equal standing* with presbyters as an order of ministry[1]. Not only does this

---

[1] In 1986 the Wesley Deaconess Order (re-named as the Methodist Diaconal Order two years later) was re-opened by the Methodist Conference as a second order of ministry (alongside presbyters) for men and women. In 1993, the MDO was recognised as an order of ministry *and* a religious order. However, not until 1998 were all ordained members of the MDO 'received into Full Connexion' by a standing vote of Conference. Staton, M. W. (2013)

'equality of ministries' need to be clearly affirmed but, in the context of mission in today's world, there needs to be a new understanding of the nature and purpose of presbyteral and diaconal ministries and their complementarity.

As juxtaposed in the *Code of Conduct*, the definitions of presbyteral and diaconal ministry have two problems. First, they differ 'in kind'. The presbyteral definition, referring to 'principal and directing', is one relating to authority (though one definition goes on to make reference to 'the (presbyteral) ministry of word, sacrament and pastoral responsibility'). However, the diaconal definition referring to 'servanthood' is one of calling or character. The issue of the 'authority' of the deacon within the Methodist Church is not addressed. Furthermore, the impression given is that, ecclesiologically, the presbyter always takes the lead role and the deacon is his or her assistant.

1.3 The definition of presbyter

1.3.1 The Deed of Union

In offering a definition of presbyteral ministry as 'principal and directing', the code extrapolates only one short phrase from the *Deed of Union* (as it currently appears in the Volume 1 of the *Constitutional Practice and Discipline of the Methodist Church*). However, the broader context [my italics] is as follows:

> Christ's ministers in the church are stewards in the household of God and shepherds of his flock. Some are called and ordained to this occupation as presbyters or deacons. Presbyters have *a principal and directing part* in these great duties *but they hold no priesthood differing in kind from that which is common to all the Lord's people and they have no exclusive title to the preaching of the gospel or the care of souls. These ministries are shared with them by others to whom also the Spirit divides his gifts severally as he wills.*
>
> *The Methodist Church holds the doctrine of the priesthood of all believers and consequently believes that no priesthood exists which belongs exclusively to a particular order or class of persons... For the sake of church order and not because of any priestly virtue inherent in the office* the presbyters of the Methodist Church are set apart by ordination to the ministry of the word and sacraments.

As noted above, the *Deed of Union* makes it clear that any 'principal and directing' ministry that presbyters have is, for Methodism, a matter of church order and not founded on any special theology of ministry. On the contrary, that theology upholds the conviction of the Methodist Church that presbyters (and indeed, deacons) hold no *priesthood differing in kind from that which is common to all the Lord's people*. Based on this statement, therefore, it needs to be emphasised that the ministries of presbyters, deacons and lay people are (theologically) of equal standing. It is a principle which stands at the heart of Methodism as a Connexional system. It also needs to be noted that, as with all matters of church order, the roles and responsibilities of presbyter and deacon are open to adaptation in the light of the changing needs and practices of secular as well as ecclesiastical life.

1.3.2 An historical anachronism

The definition of presbyteral ministry as being 'principal and directing' comes from the original draft of the *Deed of Union* of 1932. This was drawn up more than sixty years before what is now called the Methodist Diaconal Order was, in 1993, accepted by the Methodist Conference as a second order of ministry. The nature of the authority exercised by presbyter and deacon (even in the context of church order) has never been seriously reviewed since the Methodist Diaconal Order became an order of ministry. This anomaly now needs addressing.

1.3.3 'Servant leadership' and presbyteral ministry

Over recent years management theory and practice has moved away from the concept of leadership being associated with a 'directing' role, except in situations where decisions need to be taken rapidly because of the critical nature of the context (for example, in the case of the armed forces). It is the concept of 'servant leadership' which has come to the fore as good practice in many situations, secular as well as sacred.

This is especially the case where institutions have a relational rather than a purely functional task, as in the case of the church.[1] Thus, to

---

[1] A number of Christian associations engaged in exploring the contemporary nature of church leadership stress that the essence of *all* ministerial orders and offices is that of servant leadership. See for example, MODEM, a well-established ecumenical association concerned with 'ministry, management and leadership' in the church which, over the years, has published numerous books and papers on this subject.

describe presbyteral leadership as primarily exercising a 'directing' role is out of step with a mainstream understanding of leadership today. The code implicitly acknowledges this when it states that 'the conduct of the minister should be that of a loving servant' (*Ministerial Code*, Being in relationship with others – column 2) as a statement meant to apply to *all* ministers, deacons *and* presbyters.

1.3.4 *The nature and authority of presbyteral ministry*

For the reasons given above, the nature and authority of presbyteral ministry now requires critical re-appraisal in a world very different from that when the *Deed of Union* was drafted.

1.4. The definition of deacon

1.4.1 *'Witness through service'*?

For many years it was almost a cliché, as in the case of *What is a Deacon?* (2004, para 5), to describe the nature of diaconal ministry as primarily that of 'witness through service'. However, in recent years this understanding of a renewed diaconate has been called into question. For example:

o In his now well-known work on the nature of *diakonia* in the New Testament, John Collins (for example, *Diakonia Studies*, 2014) argues that the New Testament definition of that word is about one who is an agent or messenger commissioned by a person in authority, not about 'humble service'.

o *What is a Deacon?* is ambiguous. Alongside its contention that diaconal ministry is primarily 'witness through service', it also states that 'the primary purpose' of diaconal ministry is 'to help all Christians discover, develop and express their own servant ministry. Deacons therefore engage in educational and nurturing activities to enable people to see God's activity in daily life and world, and encourage them in expressing their faith in relevant ways' (Ibid., para 5.4). A ministry of service and an educational and enabling ministry are very different forms of ministry.

o It is increasingly being argued that the church must become a diaconal, or servant church, if it is to have authenticity and carry credibility in today's world.[1] Consequently, the

---

[1] See the first section of *The Jerusalem Report* (2012). See also Clark (2005).

ministry of the whole people of God, and its leadership, must also be diaconal. 'Representing the servanthood of Christ', a calling noted in *What is a Deacon?*, and assumed by the code to be at the heart of diaconal ministry, is one which should characterise the life and work of the *whole* church.

o From the days of the early church, diaconal ministry has always been the most contextual of all ministries. That is still the case. Thus it provides a useful catalyst for the church in reshaping all its ministries to make its mission relevant in this day and age.

1.4.2 Review of diaconal ministry and presbyteral ministry

It is essential that any re-appraisal of the nature and authority of diaconal ministry is undertaken alongside that of a re-appraisal of the nature and authority of presbyteral ministry. This is particularly important because, as I argue below, these two orders of ministry are complementary as well as co-equal.

2 The nature and authority of presbyteral and diaconal ministry in Methodism and the wider church[1]

2.1 The need for a mission context

There can be no sound ecclesiology unless it is based on a theology of mission. Thus identifying the nature and authority of presbyteral and diaconal ministries requires a missional context. My argument is that the context of mission today is the need for the world to become a global community of communities if it is not to succumb to the forces which threaten its survival, not least those of growing xenophobia and an introverted nationalism. I also argue that the contribution of the church to this quest is to embody and offer the gifts the kingdom community – life, liberation, love and learning – as the exemplification of community at its zenith (Clark, 2005).

2.2 The nature of leadership within the diaconal church

2.2.1 The mission of the diaconal church

---

[1] The material included in this section draws largely on Clark (2016). It is set out in a wider context in Paper 1.

The hall-mark of the diaconal church is that it is the servant of the kingdom community – as are its people and its leadership. As its mission is to call all secular institutions to a similar form of servanthood, the diaconal church also becomes a model for secular institutions. The mission of the diaconal church is to enable the latter to be transformed by the gifts of the kingdom community.

2.2.2 The laity

The laity is the primary mission resource of the diaconal church. Leadership is about nurturing, equipping and resourcing lay people for this ministry.

2.2.3 Diaconal leadership within the wider church

As the *Ministerial Code of Conduct* quite rightly states: 'Those ordained as presbyters and deacons "focus, express and enable the ministry of the whole people of God" ' [Vocation (call and commitment) – column 1]. However, as the *Deed of Union* stresses, they do so as equal partners in mission and holding 'no priesthood differing in kind from that which is common to all the Lord's people'. The Methodist Church does not accept a theology of ministry which is hierarchical in nature. Thus as a matter of theology, as well as church order, presbyter and deacon are leaders of equal standing.

The hierarchical nature of ordained ministry upheld by other churches, such as the Roman Catholic Church and the Church of England, has made the re-emergence of a permanent (or distinctive) diaconate a potential asset, but also a considerable problem. In the case of both these churches, a permanent diaconate offers a human resource badly needed in the face of a steep decline in the number of priests. However, the fact that, in both denominations, deacons are still regarded as a 'lower' order has meant that they are usually seen as assistants to the clergy, primarily in a liturgical and pastoral context.

This situation is being contested by a number of eminent people within these churches. For example, Deacon William Ditewig (formerly the Executive Director of the Secretariat for the Diaconate at the United States Conference of Catholic Bishops) argues that 'the diaconate is *not* an abridged or substitute form of priesthood, but is *a full order in its own right*' (his italics) (2007, p. 12). Unfortunately, in the Church

43

of England, and despite three well informed reports supportive of a permanent diaconate published only a few years ago,[1] its permanent diaconate remains in a subordinate position submerged by that church's historic commitment to a transitional diaconate.

Here Methodist theology and ecclesiology gives it the precious liberty to be a pioneer in the development of a renewed permanent diaconate and in the relationship of diaconal and presbyteral ministries. Such a development would not only help to reshape and re-energise the mission of Methodism as an historic mission movement but be an invaluable contribution to the universal church. What would such a development look like?

2.3 A renewed diaconate as an order of mission

Currently the Methodist Church is somewhat perplexed as to where the ministry of deacons fits into its ecclesiology and its understanding of church order. Few within the Connexion are clear as to the calling of the deacon and, as argued above, define this as 'witness through service'. The fact that within the diaconal church this is the call of every lay person does not help matters. The growing tendency to regard deacons as 'jack-of-all-trades' (including fitting into presbyteral roles where there is a lack of presbyters) simply muddies the waters further.

I believe that God is offering to the church to come the gift of a renewed diaconate as 'mission enablers'. The hall-mark of that calling is enabling, educating and equipping the people of God to exercise their ministry as *the church dispersed in the 'secular' world* (Clark, 2016, pp. 135-6) – be it at home, at work, or in pursuing leisure interests. Thus, as an order of ministry, a renewed diaconate is also *an order of mission*.

Because such a calling is about transforming secular collectives into kingdom communities, the Methodist Diaconal Order, *as a religious community*, is in a unique position to model this form of ministry. Such a leadership role does not detach the deacon from the life of the gathered church. On the contrary, it means deacons being located within the latter as their liturgical, educational and pastoral base from which to

---

[1] See *For such a time as this. A renewed diaconate in the Church of England* (2001); *Distinctive Diaconate* (2003); *The Mission and Ministry of the Whole Church* (2007).

shape and further the mission of the people of God in their engagement with the wider world.

2.3.1 Complementarity of ministries – a renewed presbyterate as an order of continuity

God's gift of a renewed form of presbyteral ministry is complementary to that of a renewed diaconate. Presbyters would become **an order of continuity** enabling *the gathered church* to manifest more fully the gifts of the kingdom community. The focus of such a calling is educating the people of God in the meaning of Christian faith, whilst supporting and enriching their lives through worship and pastoral care. In this context it is still quite appropriate to speak of presbyters as having 'pastoral charge' of the gathered church.

Continuity is in no way the same as maintenance. It is a crucial leadership task which seeks to ensure that the resources and riches of the past are employed for the fulfilment of the church in the present. It is a calling on which the resilience and ongoing life and work of the church depends. However, such a calling is also about change, ensuring that the life of the gathered church is ever more fully enriched by and manifests the gifts of the kingdom community.

Continuity is also about mission. However, in the case of presbyters, it is about their responsibility for building up and replicating the life of the gathered church. Thus 'fresh expressions of *church*' and '*church planting*' are forms of continuity in which presbyters would be actively involved.

2.4 Diaconal and presbyteral ministries as co-equal and in practice

A renewed diaconate as an order of mission and a renewed presbyterate as an order of continuity, would be not only complementary but 'full and equal orders' (Barnett) of ministry. This development calls into question the theology of a three-fold form of ministry embracing sequential ordination still espoused by a number of mainstream denominations. However, it is an understanding of leadership which I believe Methodism was called into being to offer to the church to come.

However, Methodism does not always practice what it preaches. There has in recent years been an increasing tendency, not least in conversations with the Church of England about closer relationships [see Paper 9], to clone the threefold ministerial hierarchy of the Church of England and deny the theological foundations of its own *Deed of Union*. For Methodism to get its own house in order a number of important changes in church order need to take place. I mention here two of the most symbolic and influential of these.

o Deacons should be authorized to preside at the Lord's Supper – not as a regular practice (this would remain the responsibility of presbyters) but as and when the situation was related to their calling as mission enablers. Such an occasion might be when the gathered church was giving special recognition to the ministry of the people of God in the world. It might also be when the deacon was engaged in community building well beyond the life of the gathered church as such.

o Deacons should be eligible to be nominated to serve as President of Conference or as a Chair of District. It should be noted that in the early church deacons were sometimes appointed directly to episcopal office.

I believe that unless changes of this kind are instigated, the Methodist diaconate will continue to be seen as a secondary order, its all-important calling of equipping the people of God for ministry in daily life devalued and the gift of a renewed diaconate negated.

May 2017

3 The diaconate as a new order of mission

Preamble

This paper focuses on the theology and ecclesiology underpinning the diaconate as a new order of mission. The argument of the paper is that the church to come – the diaconal church – needs a form of leadership which can enable and empower its lay people, together with fellow travellers of other faiths or none, to act as servants of the kingdom community in the world.

At present the institutional church in the UK has a form of leadership which entails presbyters (priests) trying, often at considerable threat to their own well-being, to be all things to all people. At the same time, fresh roles (such as new forms of chaplaincy, ministers in secular employment and pioneer ministers – usually filled by presbyters) are being developed haphazardly with little evidence as to how they might help or hinder the mission of the church in today's world.

My contention is that it is God's gift of a renewed diaconate, properly trained and equipped, which is in pole position to become an order of mission able to educate the people of God for their ministry in the world. In this paper I spell out the theological and ecclesiology arguments for this conviction.

1 Introduction

1.1 The dominance of 'Church-shaped mission'

It is common knowledge that all the mainstream churches in the UK are experiencing aging congregations and numerical decline. At the same time a similar clerical profile is leading to a growing shortage of presbyters (priests) within all denominations.

One response to this crisis has been to try to create 'fresh expressions of church'. Another has been to encourage 'church planting'. As a result, some signs of renewal and growth have appeared. For example, 'messy churches' have sprung up in a host of places. By adopting radical changes in their timing or style of meetings for worship or other activities, a number of congregations have managed to attract some new attenders. However, these initiatives have one significant limitation in common. They are dominantly focused on creating new forms of *church*.

The renewal of the church is of vital importance for nurturing new 'disciples' and for sustaining public awareness of the importance of Christian faith. However, so much time and energy is being expended on creating 'fresh expressions of *church*', that furthering the life and work of the kingdom, especially within a secular society, has virtually disappeared off the agenda. 'Church-shaped mission' has taken precedence over an outward looking mission-shaped church.

1.2 The transformation of society

Christ's prayer was for 'the kingdom to come on earth as it is in heaven'. This means that the mission of the church is first and foremost about the transformation of society and world. Nothing could be more crucial in this day and age when the scale of issues which face us impinge on the very future of human civilisation. If the church's primary concern is 'to seek first' the kingdom, then matters relating to the nature and form of its own survival will take care of themselves.

The kingdom is, of course, already present and constantly at work within every sector of society – from government to law and order, from finance to business, from the education of the young to life-long learning, and from health to welfare. However, the gifts of the kingdom can remain unacknowledged and wasted without a church dedicated to serve that kingdom with all the commitment and resources it can.

1.3 The liberation of the laity

It is no easy transition for a church pre-occupied with its own future to become the servant of the kingdom. An imperative first step is for the ministry of the people of God in the world to come centre stage and for them to be effectively equipped for that task. However, even as long ago as the 1960s, Mark Gibbs and Ralph Morton were arguing that the human resources available to the church for mission within society had become *God's Frozen People* (1964). Because the church has turned its attention increasingly inwards over recent decades, the task of 'unfreezing' the laity is even more challenging now than it was then.

1.4 A new order of mission

Liberating the full potential of the laity as the people of God in the world will prove extremely difficult unless it is facilitated by the creation of a new order of mission. The purpose of such an order would be to bring the ministry of lay people centre-stage and equip them to operate as servants of the kingdom throughout the whole of society. *It is my contention that a renewed diaconate is a gift of God to the church of our time and should form the core of such an order.*

This paper sets out what I see as the hall-marks of a renewed diaconate as a new order of mission. I describe these hall-marks under the headings below. In each section, I suggest ways in which the British Methodist Church, and the Methodist Diaconal Order (MDO) in particular, could take a lead in the formation of such an order.

2 The hall-marks of a new order of mission

2.1 Founded on a communal theology of the kingdom

A new order of mission would be founded on a theology which re-instates the kingdom as its primary focus. I believe that the concept of 'the kingdom', a term understandably suspect in today's world, still has the potential to offer immense impetus to the mission of the church. I also believe that such potential would be immeasurably enhanced if greater prominence were to be given to an understanding of the kingdom as 'a kingdom community' – the community of the people of God, yet one which embraces those of other faiths and convictions.

Parker Palmer, a Quaker, argued some years ago that 'community means more than the comfort of souls. It means, and has always meant, the survival of the species' (Palmer, 1987, p. 15). If he is right, a world that hopes to flourish as well as survive urgently needs a vision of community at its zenith. The kingdom as an image of an inclusive and universal community offers such a vision.

Lordship within the kingdom community is exercised by the divine community, the Trinity. The kingdom community offers to humanity what I have identified elsewhere (Clark, 2005; 2016) as the gifts of life, liberation, love and learning. It is these gifts that enable community to become a power for inclusivity and universality, not for the closure and exclusivity which is today evident in highly destructive collective forms from sectarianism to ultra-nationalism.

The Methodist Diaconal Order (MDO) has not yet produced any explicit theology of mission. However, the report *What is a Deacon?*, approved by the Methodist Conference in 2004, points to the Trinity as the model underpinning the life and work of the MDO. It states:

> God as Trinity is the model for Church life and ministry underpinning this paper. Speaking of the one God as a loving communion of three co-equal 'persons' suggests that the Church should be a community of mutual support and love in which there is no superiority or inferiority. Interdependent partners exist in a community where they lovingly interweave and also retain a distinctive individuality. The image of these three persons engaged in a dance conveys something of the dynamic involved. All Methodist people, including those in ordained ministry, are called to such a community life.

2.2 Empowered by a communal spirituality

A communal spirituality offers access to the gifts of the kingdom community. Such a spirituality would empower the people of God as they face the hard task of exercising their ministry in a secular society. I have suggested elsewhere that a communal spirituality of the kingdom could greatly benefit from drawing on the church's heritage of Celtic, Ignatian, Methodist and Quaker spirituality (Clark, 2016, pp. 29-44).

The MDO has not yet developed a distinctive communal spirituality to inform and energise its approach to mission. Its Rule of Life remains a potential foundation for this. However, at present, that rule is better adapted to enhancing the personal spirituality of deacons than to producing a common spirituality which empowers the Order's collective approach to mission.

2.3 The diaconal church and its leadership

Because the calling of the future church is to be the servant of the kingdom community, I describe it as a diaconal, or servant church. I have identified the hall-marks of the diaconal model of church in numerous publications (for example, Clark, 2005; 2008). Here I simply note that it is a model of church radically different from the Christendom model which still moulds the life and work of the mainstream denominations in the West. Because the diaconal church is the servant of the kingdom community, all its leaders would be seen as servant leaders.

A diaconal order of mission, founded on a kingdom theology of mission and a communal spirituality which earths it, would become a core form of leadership within this new model of church. At the end of this paper, I stress that a new diaconal order of mission would need to be complemented by a new presbyteral order of continuity.

I believe that the British Methodist Church and the MDO already embrace many features of the diaconal church. Because of this, both are in pole position to develop and sustain the Methodist diaconate as a new order of mission.

2.4 A transformational order of mission

A new order of mission would possess a transformational vision for the future of society. This vision would be of a society transformed by the gifts of the kingdom community – life, liberation, love and learning. It would offer an alternative to those forces which dehumanise relationships and divide society. I explore in some detail how this mission might be undertaken within the world of work in Clark (2014) *The Kingdom at Work Project*.

The most transformational understanding of the mission of a renewed diaconate published in recent years was embodied in a public statement drawn up by an ecumenical consultation, including representatives of the MDO, meeting at the latter's 'mother house' in Birmingham in 1997. This consultation set out its vision for diaconal ministry as:

> Christ-focused, people-centred and lived out in a lifestyle both active and contemplative... We increasingly perceive our role to be pioneering and prophetic, responding to needs, proactive in opportunity through commitment to mission and pastoral care

within and beyond the Church. Opening doors of opportunity, encouraging others to take risks, the contemporary diaconate acting in its capacity as 'agent of change', engages imaginatively and collaboratively with issues of justice, poverty, social and environmental concerns. We often find ourselves spanning boundaries, especially official ones of Church and society.

(The Windsor Statement on the Diaconate, 1997)

2.5 An enabling order of mission

I call the primary apostolate[1] of members of a new order of mission that of 'mission enablers'. I define that calling as one of affirming, encouraging, educating, equipping and empowering the people of God for their ministry throughout the whole of society. The acceptance of this vital leadership role would mean deacons learning to step back from a self-centred form of apostolate and acquiring the skills to bring lay people to the fore as the church's primary resource for mission within society.

The MDO continues to live with the traditional view that the focal apostolate of the diaconate is 'witness though service' (*What is a Deacon?* 5.0). Though in its origins this was an appropriate description of the diaconal calling, with the coming of the welfare state and the professionalization of social work, this vocational definition has become somewhat dated. Even more important, the mission statement 'witness through service' can all too easily give the impression that the deacon is the main exemplification of such action. This devalues the ministry of lay people who often bear 'witness through service' in equally impressive ways.

Nevertheless, there are some indications that the MDO is beginning to grasp the importance and implications of the primacy of the enabling role which would be at the heart of its apostolate as a new order of mission. I cite below examples of the MDO's slowly developing appreciation of this form of apostolate.

---

[1] I use the term 'apostolate' here and in other Papers to mean the primary calling of those called to any form of leadership within the life of the church.

The Conference report *What is a Deacon?* represents an encouraging ambivalence about the deacon's primary apostolate. On the one hand, it continues to affirm that 'witness through service' is 'the core emphasis' (op. cit. 5.0) of diaconal ministry. On the other hand, it also states that:

> 'The deacon's *primary* [my italics] role is to enable others' (3.3).
> 'Their (deacon's) particular vocation leads them into a role of leading, encouraging and enabling others' (5.1). 'Deacons therefore engage in educational and nurturing activities to enable people to see God's activity in daily life and world, and to encourage them in expressing their faith in relevant ways' (5.4).

Further evidence of a radical change in understanding of the apostolate of a renewed diaconate as a distinctive gift of God comes from Sue Jackson, a former Warden of the Order. In 2008, she wrote (Clark, 2008, p. 162):

> I believe that we are dealing with the need for a Copernican shift in people's understanding of diaconal leadership. All of us have to move from focusing on deacons as the prime agents of diaconal ministry to lay people as the crucial servants, assisted by deacons. This is as much a matter of attitudinal change in deacons themselves as in the church generally – though it does not follow a clear developmental pattern. Thus I believe that we need to attend primarily to the matter of attitude when thinking about the factors that hinder or help deacons become enablers, although I do not want to underestimate the importance of structural issues or training.

Finally, an unofficial 'mission statement', widely appreciated within the Order when it was introduced by a former Warden in 2009, describes the MDO as: 'a mission focused, pioneering religious community committed to *enabling* (my italics) outreach, evangelism and service in God's world'.

2.6 A secular apostolate – 'friends of the kingdom'

The reality faced by a diaconal church seeking to engage with a secular society is that there are now many areas of life and work in which those who call themselves Christians are thin on the ground, if in evidence at all. The church in the West, moulded by an anachronistic Christendom model, has found itself unable to engage effectively with a rapidly changing world. Consequently many congregations now have only a handful of people in full-time employment. This situation poses a huge problem for a church which is called to make the gifts of the kingdom community manifest within every sector of society.

The mainstream churches are at last beginning to acknowledge this situation and attempting to address the immense challenge it poses. However, most approaches continue to exemplify the clericalism typical of a Christendom model of church. One such approach is to assume that chaplains (and 'ministers in secular employment') can bridge the growing divide. This is wishful thinking. On the one hand, there are simply not enough of them. On the other, most see their apostolates as pastoral rather than transformative in any fundamental sense. Consequently such forms of intervention offer no alternative to what Stanley Hauerwas calls 'the grain of the world' (Martin, pp. 6-7), a culture within society which runs counter to Christian values.

A more recent attempt by the mainstream churches to engage with a secular society is through the promotion of so-called 'pioneer' ministries. However such ministers are even thinner on the ground than chaplains. Furthermore, their agenda seems to be more about 'making disciples' and 'growing the church' than the transformation of society.

The theology set out at the beginning of this paper assumes that the kingdom community is present and active in every sector of society, even where no Christians are in evidence. In this context I believe that the only realistic way forward for a church seeking to engage with today's society, is for members of a new order of mission to seek to work as 'mission enablers', not only with the laity who are at work (paid or voluntary), but with those who, though not explicitly accepting the designation 'Christian', implicitly espouse kingdom values. These may be people of other faiths or convictions.

I would call such people 'friends of the kingdom'. I believe that it is a concept which needs to be explored at much greater depth in the context of the church's mission in today's world. An important responsibility of the mission enabler would be to help all friends of the kingdom to become aware of the nature and source of the kingdom values latent, if not yet manifest in many secular contexts (Clark, 2014).

Few members of the MDO are as yet able to undertake the calling of mission enabler within church or world. For one thing, their contracts of employment are dominantly related to the needs of the gathered church and not the transformation of society. For another, the apostolate of the mission enabler in this context requires considerable experience of the working world, as well as skills of discernment and intervention. (Clark, 2016, pp. 139-323)

However, one or two deacons, in line with their calling as 'sector' ministers (deacons holding secular jobs), are attempting to fulfil this form of ministry. I myself have been engaged in a number of diaconal initiatives of this kind, such as the Human City Initiative which ran in Birmingham from 1994 to 2002 (Clark, 2012; 2016).

2.7 A common apostolate

One of the great strengths of a new order of mission would be the fact that all its members would share the calling of mission enabler. This would help in the exchange of experiences, insights and resources in a self-critical yet supportive way. Such a common apostolate would be especially important if members of the new order were widely dispersed or working in isolated situations.

Methodist deacons already have a strong sense of solidarity. This would be further enhanced if their apostolate possessed a clearer common focus. I believe that becoming a new order of mission would offer a new and exciting challenge, strengthen commitment and attract new members to the Methodist Diaconal Order.

A mission-oriented and common apostolate of this kind would also enable diaconal training, pre- and post-ordination, to be more distinctive. It would facilitate a more creative sharing of experiences and insights in area groups and Convocation.

2.8 A religious order

A new order of mission would be greatly strengthened by being a religious order. On the one hand, its sense of community would be enhanced by its members having a common Rule of Life. On the other hand, what it means to facilitate the building of kingdom communities would be exemplified by its daily experience as a community of life and practice.

The MDO is one of the few diaconal associations to be formally recognised as a religious order by its own church. Its Rule of Life, including praying for one another and mutual pastoral support in area groups, already bonds the Order strongly together. The experience of being a religious order also offers encouragement to Methodist deacons as they seek to fulfil their apostolates in widely scattered locations. When published in 2004, *What is a Deacon?* assumed the experience of MDO as an order of ministry *and* as a religious order to be 'completely intertwined' (3.5). If the MDO developed into an order of mission, its experience as a religious order would give its community building apostolate even greater impetus and sense of direction.

The integration of the MDO as an order of ministry and a religious order places it in pole position to demonstrate to a much wider constituency what a new order of mission could offer church and society.

2.9 In partnership with a 'third order'

A number of religious orders, with the Franciscans pre-eminent, have set up 'third orders' of lay people who 'associate' themselves with the life and work of that order. This gives the order encouragement and support in a diversity of ways. It also inspires members of the third order to engage in a life-style which not only models the form of a Franciscan apostolate but supports its own members in their daily life and work.

As yet the MDO does not have a 'third order' supporting it. It has a number of 'associates'. However, these are often former deacons who, having moved into presbyteral ministry, wish to maintain a personal link with the order. If the MDO became a new order of mission, I believe it would benefit greatly from the support and encouragement of a third order of lay people who had a similar missional commitment to the communal transformation of society. [This matter is discussed more fully in Paper 7.]

June 2017

4 The calling of the deacon as mission enabler

Preamble

In Paper 3, I focused on the nature and potential of the diaconate as a new order of mission. I argued that in the coming diaconal church, diaconal and presbyteral orders should be seen as complementary and of equal standing. I also argued that the calling of a renewed diaconate was a gift of God to our time which could best be described as that of 'mission enablers'. However, I am aware that, in practice, this term currently encompasses a confusing variety of roles. In this paper, therefore, I explore more fully what I mean by the term 'mission enabler' when used to describe the primary calling and responsibilities of a new diaconal order of mission.

1 The meaning of mission

As currently used in the church, the term 'mission enabler' is employed to cover such a diversity of roles that it has come to mean virtually all things to all people. Thus, in defining the meaning of that term for the ministry of a renewed diaconate, the only way forward is to begin by recapping on what I mean by 'mission' and, then, to describe the calling of the deacon as 'enabler' in that context.

1.1 The mission task – building kingdom communities

My earlier articles have set the mission of the church in the context of a world urgently needing to discover what it means to be a global community. My thesis is that humanity now faces some of the most profound challenges it has ever experienced, from the misuse of weapons of mass destruction to imminent global climate change. At the same time, the rise of autocracy, racism and xenophobia threatens to destroy any hope of humankind addressing these issues as a global community of communities.

In this context, the mission of the church must be primarily focused on offering humanity a vision of community which can inspire and sustain it, and the power to make that vision a reality. This task I see as pointing humankind, collectively and individually, to the

Trinity, as embodying the meaning of community, and to the concept of the kingdom as what that community looks like when earthed in everyday life. I call this vision that of the kingdom community with its Trinitarian gifts of life, liberation, love and learning (Clark, 2005). Thus the mission of the church in our day and age is to build kingdom communities which manifest these gifts within every sector of society.

This mission will include the 'making of disciples'. However, it is nowhere near enough for mission to be concerned with the salvation of individuals. A world seeking to survive another millennium needs a far bigger vision of mission. It requires a church working to make the gifts of the kingdom community manifest within every human collective from the family to the nation and beyond.

1.2 The diaconal church

The West has inherited a Christendom model of church from a very different era and with a very different mission. Therefore, it is no wonder that it is struggling not only to survive numerically but, far more important, in terms of credibility and authority. My argument is that the mould of Christendom must be broken and another model of church has to come into being. I call the model of the church now needed 'the diaconal' or servant church'. It is a church which is the servant, first, of the kingdom community and, then, secondly, of humankind. Because the medium must be the message, it is imperative that the diaconal church makes manifest the gifts of life, liberation, love and learning within and through every aspect of its own life and work.

1.3 The laity as the diaconal church's primary mission resource

Within the diaconal church, lay people are the primary missionary resource. They are the servants of the kingdom. They are its eyes, hands and feet within daily life. It is essential that they are liberated from dependency on clerical leadership, typical of the Christendom model of church, if they are to engage in any realistic and effective way with the issues facing today's world.

The engagement of lay people within society has two main aspects. The first task is to discern the signs of the kingdom community in whatever situation they find themselves.[1] This requires a range of skills from personal experience of the gifts of the kingdom community to those of awareness and observation. The second task is to intervene in the situation concerned to bring the gifts of the kingdom community to the fore. This may mean affirmation of positive evidence of the gifts of the kingdom community at work or challenging practices which lead to those gifts being ignored or negated. Intervention may be undertaken individually, or in partnership with others, whether Christian or of other convictions. Intervention may be explicit (making open reference to the Christian motivation for such intervention) or implicitly (where the Christian impetus for intervention is allowed to speak for itself).

This description of mission as a matter of discernment and intervention identifies the hall-marks of a process which is often spontaneous and unconscious. In practice, discernment and intervention will frequently be more piece-meal and ad hoc than suggested above. Nevertheless, it is important for lay people to be aware of key aspects of an overall process which needs to be at the heart of mission if the church's quest for the communal transformation of society is to be more than wishful thinking.

1.4 The leadership of the diaconal church

A key feature of the diaconal church is a new form of leadership shaped by a kingdom theology of mission and a diaconal ecclesiology. Here leadership takes the form of servant leadership, in both the biblical and, more recently, secular sense (Greenleaf, 1970). The leaders of the diaconal church are servants of the kingdom community and its gifts, servants of the laity and servants of humankind.

The offices and titles of deacon, presbyter (priest) and bishop may be retained within the diaconal church. However, they are dispensable titles. Within such a church, any three-fold form of leadership is made up of 'full and equal orders' (Barnett, 1995). It is in no theological or ecclesiological sense hierarchical.

---

[1] With respect to the ministry of Christians at work, see Clark (2014) *The Kingdom at Work Project*. This is a key text with regards to the art of discernment and the process of intervention. Much of the text can be applied to situations beyond the world of work.

In the diaconal church, the calling of presbyters is to the continuity of the inherited gathered church. This is far removed from maintenance. Continuity is about drawing on the experience and lessons of the past to enhance the future. It embraces development and mission in order to further 'fresh expressions of *church*' as well as *church* growth in general. However, across all facets of this calling, the presbyter's foundational task is to enable the gathered church, inherited or as a fresh expression, to manifest the gifts of the kingdom community.

The responsibility of the bishop is to support, nurture, integrate and help resource the ministries of presbyter and deacon, and the laity whom they serve.

1.5 The leadership role of a renewed diaconate

A renewed diaconate is a gift of God to the church of our time. Its calling is to animate and equip the laity, the diaconal church dispersed in the world, to help collectives within every sector of society – from the family to education, from health to welfare, from business to industry, from law and order to government – to manifest the gifts of the kingdom community. It is a leadership role which has over the centuries been consigned to the back burner of the Christendom model of church. However, it is a role which urgently needs to come to the fore if the church is to engage in a meaningful way with the world of the twenty-first century.

2 The deacon as enabler

2.1 From service to enabling

The calling of the diaconate has always been contextual. Of all the leadership offices within the church, it is the diaconate which has been the most tenacious yet flexible in adapting to the needs of the age. Thus the revival of the diaconate during the industrial revolution was given impetus by the need for the church to respond to the poverty and deprivation caused by mass migration to the cities and a lack of healthy places of work, decent housing and good sanitation. 'Witness through service' was quite properly a mission statement guiding the vocation of the diaconal associations at this time.

However, with the coming of the welfare state, a National Health Service, universal education and greater opportunities for women to enter a wide range of professions, the role of the deacon again became ambivalent. 'Witness through service' came to be regarded as the responsibility of the whole church and, as Paul Avis argues, a ministry which 'all Christians are meant to do all the time' (2013, 2:2.8). It is not surprising, therefore, that both the Church of England and the British Methodist Church came to the conclusion that diaconal ministry was now superfluous and attempted to end recruitment to that office. However, both attempts at closure eventually failed, not least because many members of both churches retained faith in the diaconate as an important leadership resource and its potential to adapt to changing needs.

Over recent decades, the vocation of a renewed diaconate, at least in the West, has become clearer. In the light of the theology and ecclesiology set out above, the core task of a future diaconate is to enable lay people to fulfil the mission of the servant, or diaconal church. This means equipping the people of God to become kingdom community builders within every sector of society. It is a vital calling but one which will only emerge as the diaconate experiences what Sue Jackson, a former Warden of the Methodist Diaconal Order, calls 'a Copernican revolution'(Clark, 2008, p. 162) in awareness, training and practice.

2.2 A renewed diaconate's enabling role

Fulfilling the role and responsibilities of enabler is a considerable art. It does not come naturally because for most deacons doing is far easier than enabling. This is why the traditional vocation of witness through service is in many ways much easier to fulfil than the more self-effacing calling of mission enabler. The latter requires a range of attitudes, abilities and skills which take a great deal of time and experience to acquire.

The enabling role is likely to involve the deacon in any number of the following tasks:

o helping lay people to become aware of the nature and mission of the diaconal church;

o fostering lay people's ability to discern the kingdom community's gifts of life, liberation, love and learning in everyday life;

61

o enabling lay people to use their skills of discernment to shape their mission task;

o animating and enthusing lay people for that task;

o working with lay people to design a strategy for intervention;

o equipping lay people with the knowledge and skills to fulfil their mission task.

o equipping lay people with the skills to create partnerships with those – whether Christian or not – who might offer assistance with the mission task. This may involve enabling lay people to draw on any relevant experience of members of the gathered church with which they are associated.

o enabling lay people to gain access to and employ resources which might be required to fulfil their mission task;

o enabling lay people to evaluate and learn from the effectiveness or otherwise of their intervention.

The role of enabler may also mean the deacon becoming a mentor[1] of lay people, individually or as a group.

2.3 Training mission enablers

A number of Methodist deacons are already exercising a role which is essentially that of mission enabler.[2] Using their natural abilities, many are fulfilling this role extremely well. However, for the diaconate as whole to be able to fulfil the responsibilities of mission enablers, deacons will need a form of training not yet on offer. Some years ago, I attempted to set out the kind of knowledge and skills needed for this role in *The Formation and Training of Deacons* (Clark, November 2008)[3]. In this document I described the role of mission enabler as that of 'community educator'. However, in practice, the two roles are very similar. In addition to the core skills of enabling and education I listed, were those of relationship building, communication, being a change

---

[1] The nature of mentoring is discussed more fully in Clark (2014).

[2] For example, in the Peak Circuit of the British Methodist Church, an enabling role is currently (2018) being fulfilled by a deacon appointed as the Peak Park Rural Development Enabler.

[3] This document received helpful comments from the then existing Methodist training institutions to which it was circulated. However, it was eventually shelved as the Order did not feel that the time was right, for the Methodist Church, as well as for the Order itself, for diaconal training to undergo a radical change of direction.

agent and an intermediary, as well as other skills including mentoring and group work.

2.4 The diaconate as representatives

As an order of mission, a renewed diaconate would give expression to, and represent the diaconal church as a movement. This would complement the responsibility of presbyters, as an order of continuity, to represent the diaconal church as an institution. The church needs to be both institution *and* movement to fulfil its diaconal calling in this day and age.

2.5 The diaconate as a religious order

The British Methodist Diaconal Order is unusual amongst diaconal associations in that is it both an order of ministry and a religious order. The latter adds value to the life and work of Methodist deacons in several important ways (Clark, 2016, 173-184). First, its Rule of Life connects and supports deacons as members of an order widely dispersed across the country. Secondly, as a religious community, the Order is able to model, for church and world, what it means to be a kingdom community and how the latter's gifts – life, liberation, love and learning – can be accessed and employed. These 'additional' attributes will be of immense value to the Methodist diaconate when it fully develops as an order of mission.

2.6 The calling of deacon as mission enabler within the world of work

The Methodist deacon as mission enabler looks to the circuit as his or her home-base. However, from that base, the calling of a renewed diaconate relates especially closely to lay people at work, either earning a living through their employment[1] or active in voluntary work. Engagement with the world of work is an aspect of ministry and mission has been neglected by the church for far too long, yet it remains one of the most influential in shaping the life of our society.

This means that deacons as mission enablers will frequently be itinerant, in the sense of travelling to connect with and help further the mission of the laity as kingdom community builders within the workplace. Deacons as mission enablers need to be well acquainted with the kind of challenges lay people face when seeking to witness to

---

[1] For a comprehensive review of what lay ministry at work involves see Clark (2014) *The Kingdom at Work Project*.

their faith at work. This means keeping abreast of current developments which are relevant to the communal transformation of the working world. It entails finding time for visiting those places where lay people work. It will also involve deacons in convening groups of lay people, on or away from church premises, to share experiences of how their faith may guide their witness in the working world.

It should be stressed that the calling of mission enabler in the world of work is very different, theologically and ecclesiologically, from that of chaplain. Normatively, the chaplain is regarded as the representative of the institutional church within the workplace. His or her role has become predominantly pastoral. In contrast, the task of the deacon as mission enabler is equipping those Christians *already present* in the world of work to become catalysts for the creation of workplaces which manifest the gifts of the kingdom community. The chaplaincy role remains largely shaped, and constrained by the Christendom model of church. The role of deacon as mission enabler is shaped by the missiology of the diaconal church.

2.7 The deacon as a team ministry member

Members of a renewed diaconate would form an important and integral part of the circuit team. The most efficient use of diaconal resources would probably be for one deacon to be appointed to each large circuit. It is likely that a presbyter, having a ministry focused primarily on the gathered church, would be team leader, with the deacon as a full and equal member of the team.

The deacon's role in worship would be focused on raising the awareness of the gathered church as a whole to the importance of mission focused on the transformation of society. Deacons would be authorized to preside at holy communion beyond as well as within the walls of the church. This would help to demonstrate that the Eucharist is a sacrament as relevant to the life of society as to that of the gathered church. The deacon might also commission the congregation, when dispersing into the world, to remember their calling as kingdom community builders in daily life.[1]

---

[1] Within the Church of England and Roman Catholic Church, deacons are being designated an increasingly active role in the liturgy, an example which Methodism could do well to emulate.

Within the gathered church, deacons as mission enablers would have special responsibility for the educating and equipping lay people for their community building ministry not only in the world of work but in daily life as a whole. They would also seek to ensure that those so engaged had the pastoral support needed to enable them to sustain their ministry in sometimes difficult circumstances.

3 The diaconal mission enabler as intermediary

The reality of the life of the mainstream churches in the West is that of steep numerical decline and an increasingly elderly age profile. This means that the church today is seeking to engage with many sectors of society in which lay people, its primary mission resource, are few and far between. Thus deacons, as mission enablers, may well find themselves with nobody 'out there' to enable. In this situation, the church has a number of choices.

One is to rely on chaplains to represent the church in the workplace. However, as noted in 2.6, most chaplaincies reflect a Christendom model of church and give priority to a dominantly pastoral role. Their ministry is rarely concerned with the radical transformation of the workplace. Furthermore, and pragmatically, the number of chaplains is tiny in comparison with the human resources needed to enable the church to fulfil its mission in the wider world. With Christians sparse on the ground, therefore, where can the diaconal church look for the human resources needed to fulfil its mission?

I believe that the way forward must be for the church to recognise that there are millions of people, other than those who would call themselves Christians, who embrace a faith or convictions which commit them to the communal transformation of society. I believe such people are those whom Christ once spoke of as being 'not far from the kingdom'. I have elsewhere called them 'friends of the kingdom' (see Paper 3, 2.6). There is no way society will ever be communally transformed unless Christians enter into partnership with such people and together seek to build human collectives which manifest the gifts of the kingdom community – life, liberation, love and learning.

In these situations the church needs to see the calling of the diaconate as mission enablers as embracing that of intermediary. The role of the latter is to seek out friends of the kingdom. It is to build bridges between the latter, lay Christians at work and, where possible, the gathered church. It is then to engage all parties in bringing the gifts of the kingdom community to the fore, whatever names these parties or gifts may be given by those involved, for the communal transformation of every human collective. As one example of such an endeavour, I draw attention to Birmingham's Human City Initiative (Clark, 2012), in which I was involved some years ago.

4 The growth of the diaconate as an order of mission

4.1 Where the churches stand

For the church to respond to the gift of a renewed diaconate as mission enablers many more deacons with a wide range of experience and skills will be required. At present (2018) the strength of the diaconate in the Church of England, with just over 100 active deacons, and the British Methodist Church[1], with 127 active deacons, is quite inadequate as a response to God's calling into being of a renewed diaconate. Compare these figures with those of the Episcopal Church of North America and Canada, with over 3000 deacons and over 200 in training, and the United Methodist Church in the USA, with over 2000 active deacons, and one realises the failure of the British churches to grasp the meaning and potential of a renewed diaconate.

The size of the diaconate in the British churches could be increased in a number of ways. All those currently employed to undertake ministries which are entitled or, in practice, resemble the role of 'mission enabler', could be encouraged to consider offering for the diaconal order. Presbyters currently engaged in ministries beyond the gathered church, such as chaplains with a more radical brief, and pioneer ministers, could likewise be encouraged to consider becoming members of a renewed diaconate. Recruitment from these quarters may not enable a renewed diaconate to reach the critical mass required for effectively operating as an order of mission throughout the church, but it would begin to offer a new order of mission the experience, skills and resources needed.

One further source of recruitment needs to be given serious attention, that of the self-supporting deacons. Many deacons across the world, including North America and Canada, are self-supporting. This

---

[1] As at July 2018 – diaconal Report to the Methodist Conference

is to be welcomed. It is a situation which keeps a renewed diaconate closely in touch with the world of work. However, one problem here is that such deacons can often interpret their paid employment as defining and delimiting their diaconal calling. The danger is, as I have argued above (2.1), that the diaconal calling is then regarded primarily as individual 'witness through service' rather than one which enables and equips lay people for their ministry in public life. Even if a self-supporting deacon is committed to a mission enabling role, the time and energy to give to it are inevitable limited.

Nevertheless, I believe a strategy for strengthening the leadership of the diaconal church is to welcome many more self-supporting deacons. In any recruitment process, they should be encouraged to see their vocation as not only concerned with their own paid work, but as educating lay people for the mission of the church in the world. In Britain, such a development would add vital experience, expertise and energy to a new diaconal order of mission.

August 2017

5 The Methodist Diaconal Order as a religious order

Preamble

The Methodist Diaconal Order was the offspring of the Wesley Deaconess Order which was widely regarded by Methodism as a form of religious order. The Order closed in 1978 but was re-opened, to men as well as women, in 1986. In 1988 it was renamed the Methodist Diaconal Order. In 1993 it was recognized by the Methodist Conference as both an order of ministry *and* a religious order. However, questions were raised from time to time as to what being a religious order meant in practice. In 2004, *What is a Deacon?*, a report approved by the Methodist Conference, described the features which the MDO regarded as giving it the character of a religious order.

Throughout this book, I argue that being a religious order is not just something which gives the members of the Methodist Diaconal Order a sense of solidarity and encouragement. It also models for church and world what it means to be a kingdom community, being a servant of which is the primary purpose of the diaconal church. Thus the medium (the MDO) is also the message.

Paper 5 has two main purposes. The first is to spell out in fuller detail the meaning and positive aspects of the MDO being a religious order. The second is to respond to two Resolutions[1] brought by the Faith and Order Committee to the Methodist Conference of 2016 in its Interim Report which, if approved, could significantly change the character of the MDO as a religious order.

---

[1] **Resolution 32/2**
The Conference directs the Methodist Council, with the Methodist Diaconal Order and the Faith and Order Committee, to consider whether the religious order should be opened to receive into membership Methodists who are lay or ordained to presbyteral ministry and report to the 2018 Conference.
Resolution 33/3
The Conference directs the Methodist Council, with the Methodist Diaconal Order and the Faith and Order Committee, to consider whether those whom it ordains to the diaconal order of ministry continue to be required also to become members of the religious order and report to the 2018 Conference.

In order to undertake the first purpose, it is necessary to look briefly at the nature of the historic religious orders, the features of early Methodism which reflect those of a religious order, the history of the Methodist deaconess associations and the origins and development of the Methodist Diaconal Order as a religious order and an order of ministry. It is only against this background that the two Resolutions of the Interim Report can be usefully evaluated. Those who wish to read the commentary explicitly concerned with the two Resolutions of the Interim Report should turn to Section 5.

1 Background to the historic religious orders

1.1 The historic calling of religious orders

Religious orders have been a feature of the church ever since it became institutionalized. They have usually come into being for one or more of the following reasons:

  o to undertake a particular apostolate (calling) which the church has neglected or been slow to address;
  o to remind the church of its call to manifest and promote holiness and justice by the quality of its member's lives – individually and collectively;
  o to offer people time and space to offer a ministry of prayer for church and world.

The reason which has most often led to the emergence of a religious order is the first of those listed above. A charismatic figure, often coming to Christian faith as a result of a personal crisis in their life, has become aware of a need which the church of the day is failing to address with commitment or consistency. For example, Benedict wished to demonstrate to the church how Christian faith could be expressed though a deeply communal way of life. The Franciscans emerged because Francis became convinced of the need to preach the good news of the kingdom to all by example and not just word. For him, this entailed his Order making a commitment to poverty so that the nature of the kingdom could be made manifest in practice. Dominic believed that a new type of organization was required to address the spiritual needs of his era, a body that would combine dedication and systematic education, with more organizational flexibility than could be offered by the monastic orders or the secular clergy of his day. His followers thus became a preaching and educational Order.

After a lull for a number of centuries, in part created by a church consumed by the Reformation and its aftermath, the nineteenth century saw the emergence of new religious orders. This was in large part due to the commitment of their founders to a new apostolate to tackle the acute needs of the poor and destitute in the burgeoning cities of the industrial revolution then transforming Europe.

1.2 The relation of religious orders to the church as an institution

Religious orders often had an ambiguous relationship to the institutional church. Institutional church leaders were afraid that some religious orders, not least because of the charismatic nature of their founders, would undermine their authority. Hence there was sometimes a long struggle before religious orders could gain acceptance by the ecclesiastical hierarchy. For example, the Society of Jesus (Jesuits), whose original apostolate was to counter the teaching of the Reformation, was suppressed by the Pope in 1773 and only opened again in 1814. Nevertheless, many church leaders recognized that religious orders, as movements with distinctive apostolates, were committed, focused and flexible enough to meet the needs of the time which the church as an institution was often too inflexible or slow to address.

2 Methodism as a religious order

2.1 Methodism as a religious order

In many respects, Methodism in its early days took on the character and form of a religious order. For example:

- o it had a charismatic leader
- o it had an apostolate focused on reaching those whom the institutional church had neglected or ignored
- o it proclaimed a life-changing message
- o its preachers were itinerant
- o its followers came together in strong bonded groups (classes and bands) to form small but linked 'societies'
- o its members committed themselves to a disciplined rule of life (set out on the class ticket).

71

However, unlike most religious orders, Methodism's apostolate and message was personal yet all-embracing. It attracted a large number of working people spread out across the country who were alienated from a moribund Church of England. Methodism's followers were deeply committed but few gave up their occupations to join the movement. A good deal of their time and energy remained consumed in the task of survival in a day and age when people's life-span was often curtailed by poverty and ill-health. Not least, early Methodism sought, but failed, to get the blessing of the Established Church.

Consequently, as the years passed, Methodism (in its different 'Connexional' forms) increasingly abandoned those features of its life typifying a religious order, assumed the characteristics of a denomination and, especially after 'union' in 1932, of a national institution in its own right. This ensured continuity and stability. However, in the process, Methodism lost the flexibility to respond to cultural and social changes, in the twentieth century of an especially rapid and far-reaching nature.

2.2 The Methodist deaconess orders

One exception to Methodism's development as an institution was the emergence of the Methodist deaconess orders in the mid-nineteenth century. As with many other such associations and orders of this era, the Methodist deaconess associations came into being to meet the acute social needs of the rapidly growing cities of the Industrial Revolution, with their squalid living conditions and totally inadequate medical care, welfare provision and education for a majority of the population.

In 1869, the Rev Thomas Bowman Stephenson founded the Children's Home (later called the National Children's Home and Orphanage and, more recently, Action for Children). He was greatly influenced by the work of Pastor Theodore Fliedner, the founder of a Lutheran deaconess community, in 1836, in Kaiserswerth, Germany. In 1878, Bowman recruited women to work for the Children's Home as Sisters of the Children. This initiative triggered the idea of an order of women employed in three main fields: moral and spiritual education; ministry to the sick poor; and evangelism.

It was not long before the United Methodist Church and the Primitive Methodist Church set up similar associations of sisters or deaconesses. The work developed rapidly. In 1901, the Wesleyan deaconesses were officially 'recognized' as a distinctive form of lay ministry by the Wesleyan Methodist Conference. In 1902, a Wesley Deaconess Institute College was founded in Ilkley to provide accommodation and training facilities for 27 students. By 1907, there were 98 fully trained Wesleyan deaconesses, 56 probationers and 19 accepted for training (Lloyd, 2010, p. 249).

To support the apostolate of the Wesley Deaconess Order, Bowman fostered their life as a religious community. He set down three principles which in time became a classic frame of reference for the Order (Graham, 2002, p. 241):

> There should be vocation but no vow...
> There should be discipline but not servility...
> There should be association but it should not exclude freedom...

However, in time all the different Methodist associations of deaconesses adopted some form of collective discipline and came to regard themselves as religious communities.

1932 saw the unification of Wesleyan Methodism, the United Methodist Church and Primitive Methodism. Within two years the deaconess associations of all these remaining branches of Methodism came together under the title of the Wesley Deaconess Order. Overall this then had a membership of some 370 deaconesses (Graham, p. 353).

The post Second World War years saw considerable fluctuations in the life and work of the Wesley Deaconess Order. Its rule of life remained consistently strong. However, its apostolate was greatly influenced by the coming of the Welfare State, not least a National Health Service, a universal education system and increasing affluence. Its ministry of 'witness through service' was increasingly taken over by secular bodies and deaconesses found themselves becoming jacks-of-all-trades. The decision by the Methodist Church to ordain women to presbyteral ministry from 1974 meant another challenge to the survival of the Order. As a result, in 1978, the Methodist Conference decided to close the Order.

2.3 The origins of the Methodist Diaconal Order

Methodism was taken by surprise when the idea of a religious order with an apostolate to address the changing needs of the wider world continued to retain its resilience. Thus, in 1986, the Methodist Conference agreed to the re-opening of what, after 1988, was called the Methodist Diaconal Order (MDO), now available to both men and women. In 1987, the first deacons were ordained into that Order.

In 1993, the Methodist Conference recognized the MDO as an order of ministry and religious order, thus acknowledging its historic continuity with the Wesley Deaconess Order. All deacons were eventually received into 'Full Connexion' in 1998. In 2004, Conference accepted the report *What is a Deacon?* as a description of the life and work of the MDO as an order of ministry and a religious order.

3 The future of the MDO as an order of ministry and a religious order[1]

3.1 *What is a Deacon?*

What is a Deacon? (2004) is the most recent attempt to identify the nature and features of the MDO as an order of ministry and religious order. It has much to commend it, in particular its 'feel' for the ethos and dynamism of the Order.

3.2 An order of ministry

Nevertheless, when it comes to identifying the 'primary' purpose (apostolate) of the MDO *as an order of ministry*, *What is a Deacon?* is ambivalent. On the one hand, the document states that 'the *core* emphasis'[2] of diaconal ministry is 'witness through service' (para 5). Yet elsewhere (para 5.4) the report contends that 'the *primary* purpose'[3] of diaconal ministry is 'to help all Christians discover, develop and express their own servant ministry. Deacons therefore engage in educational and nurturing activities to enable people to see God's activity in daily life and world, and encourage them in expressing their faith in relevant ways'.

A ministry of service and an educational and enabling ministry are very different forms of ministry. Whichever is given precedence not only has an impact on how deacons interpret their role and use their

---

[1] I explore the content of this section in greater detail in Clark (2016)
[2] My italics
[3] My italics

time and energy but, just as important, on the expectations of those who employ them. Consequently, clarification of what constitutes the MDO's current apostolate is becoming increasingly urgent.

3.3 A religious order

On the other hand, there is no ambiguity or uncertainly in *What is a Deacon?* about the nature and form of the MDO *as a religious order*. The document spends a good deal of time carefully spelling out the importance and characteristics of the latter, at the heart of which is the Order's Rule of Life, its prayer manual covering all members of the Order and its area meetings.

There is, however, something, more difficult to define, which characterizes the MDO as a religious order. Originating in the days of the Wesley Deaconess Order, there exists a deep sense of colleagueship and commitment to mutual caring and support which, in a host of small but significant ways, gives members a deep sense of significance and solidarity. For example, the annual Convocation of the Order is not just a formal gathering for worship, study and business but an occasion for the renewal of friendships and the strengthening of comradeship. That one of its hall-marks is a great deal of fun and laughter says a lot about the ethos and dynamism of the Order.

3.4 'Completely intertwined'

What is a Deacon? states that the MDO's life and work as a religious order and as an order of ministry are, and need to remain 'completely intertwined' (para 5.2). One only has to belong to the Order for a short time to experience how deeply this 'intertwining' is felt by deacons, in practice as well as in principle. It is the MDO's life as a religious order which powerfully supports and energises its apostolate as an order of ministry and, as I argue throughout this book, as an order of mission.

3.5 A 'renewed' diaconate as a new order of mission

I have spelt out in some detail elsewhere (Clark, 2016) how the diaconate in many countries, especially in the West, is now searching for a new form of apostolate so that it can better respond to the needs of a world facing the threat of weapons of mass destruction, climate change and a world population forced to be on the move as never before. That situation, symbolized by such things as Brexit, the rise of popularism in Europe and the Trump phenomenon in the USA, highlights many of the challenges we now face. Humankind has to learn quickly how to live together as a global community of communities or it will self-destruct.

In this critical context, the mission of the church has to be that of helping to build what I call 'kingdom communities' (Clark, 2005). I believe that these have the potential to model and exemplify, within every form of collective from the family to the nation and beyond, what community at its zenith really means. Such a mission needs to draw on the gifts of the kingdom community – life, liberation love and learning – each gift gaining its authenticity and power from the divine community, the Trinity. Such a kingdom community building task can only be accomplished through the church's primary mission resource – its laity.

For this undertaking, lay people need to be passionate about their calling as kingdom community builders, to be given adequate training to carry it out, to have time and energy to attend to it, and to be open and flexible enough to respond to the specific needs of the situations in which they finds themselves. To enable lay people to be equipped and ready for this kind of ministry, a new form of church leadership is urgently required.

I am convinced that such leadership can only come from God's gift of a renewed diaconate as a ***new order of mission***. This transformation will entail deacons moving away from their traditional role of 'witness through service' and, more recently, of a fragmented apostolate attempting to be all things to all people. A diaconal order of mission will, instead, focus its calling, training and apostolate on enabling the people of God to become kingdom community builders throughout every sector of society.

This is a radical change for the 'old' diaconate, at present a form of church leadership often operating on the fringes of the church, to undergo. However, down the ages the diaconate has been the most world-focused and adaptable of all forms of church leadership. It is the emergence of a new kind of diaconal leadership that will enable the church in the West to make a significant contribution to the communal well-being of society and world.

3.6 The relation of British Methodism to the diaconate as a new order of mission

Ongoing decline over recent decades means that the British Methodist Church now has a relatively minor presence on the British church scene. Nevertheless, there are a number of factors which give it a unique opportunity to pioneer the creation of the permanent diaconate as an order of mission. Such an initiative would be a very important contribution to the church of the future, the diaconal church, within the UK and beyond.

Methodism's pole position in this regard stems from a number of factors including the following:

o Its roots lie in being a new movement for the spreading of Christian holiness [see Appendix] and justice, not tied to the forms and structures of the Established Church.

o The Methodist Diaconal Order as an order of ministry is, in principle, accepted as a co-equal form of church leadership alongside that of presbyters. Methodism has never espoused a hierarchical three-fold theology of ministry which sees the diaconate as merely transitional and simply a short step towards the priesthood.

o Methodism has always regarded the ministry of the laity as a primary resource for the fulfilment of the mission of the church in the world.

o Within Methodism, the relationship of presbyters, deacons and laity is a matter of church order. Church order should reflect the needs of both church and society and should be adaptable whenever the focus and form of mission needs to be reshaped.

Methodism is in the privileged position of having the opportunity to develop the ministry of the MDO as an order of mission, a new form of church leadership of great importance for the mission of the whole Connexion, and for that of other churches in the UK and beyond.

3.7 The importance of the MDO as a religious order for its apostolate as a new order of mission

Early Methodism was not only a holiness movement but benefited greatly from possessing many features of a religious order. Its original apostolate was thus supported and energised by the commitment and solidarity of its members developed within class meetings and local societies alike. In a not dissimilar way today, the apostolate of the MDO is supported and energised by deacons being members of a religious order.

However, if, in time, the apostolate of the MDO became that of an order of mission, focused on facilitating the building of kingdom communities in society and world, then its life as a religious order, which bears witness to the meaning and nature of the kingdom community, would be an even greater asset. Being a religious community would not only continue to nourish and support deacons in their daily work, but offer a living model of the kingdom community to church and world. As such it would be an invaluable example and resource for the ministry of lay people engaged in kingdom community building within society.

4 A 'renewed presbyterate' as an order of continuity

4.1 Complementary ministries

We have learnt over recent years that church leaders need to work as teams. In this context, the ministry of deacons and presbyters must be complementary as well as co-equal. Thus no renewed diaconate and new diaconal order of mission can ultimately come into being unless a renewed form of presbyteral leadership also emerges. What might the latter look like?

As with a renewed diaconate, future presbyteral ministry needs to be shaped by a new theology and ecclesiology of mission. As argued above, a theology of mission for our time should be that of enabling every sphere of the life of society to be transformed by the gifts of the kingdom community. The church, and its leadership, is the servant of that community. The calling of a renewed diaconate is to facilitate, through the church *dispersed* in the world, the building of the kingdom community within society. I believe that the complementary calling of the presbyter is to help further that mission by enabling the *gathered* church to manifest the gifts of the kingdom community.

To this end, a renewed presbyterate would become *an order of continuity*. Such an apostolate is not about church 'maintenance'. It is about enabling the gathered church to draw on the gifts of the kingdom community as manifest within the historic churches down the ages. It is also about presbyters enabling, educating and equipping the people of God to manifest the gifts of the kingdom community in and through the life of the gathered church.

This in no way excludes presbyters from engaging in mission. However, in their case, attention would be primarily focused on the planting of new (gathered) churches and/or promoting fresh expressions of (gathered) church, albeit always seeking to enable them to exemplify the gifts of the kingdom community.

5 Consideration of the Interim Report's Resolutions

5.1 The choice of Resolutions

At the conclusion of its Interim Report, the Faith and Order Committee's working party, appended two Resolutions, further consideration of which was agreed by the Methodist Conference of 2016. However, a major difficulty in any discussion of these Resolutions is that, while the Interim Report touches on matters relating to their content, it does not explain why these particular Resolutions were chosen. There are many other important questions discussed in the Interim Report concerning the contribution of the MDO to the future of Methodism and the wider church which could have become equally significant Resolutions. Thus, as was the case for the Convocation of the MDO in 2016, those considering the raison d'être for these Resolutions begin without any background briefing.

It is my conviction that before the two Resolutions concerned can be addressed in an informed and creative way there needs to be:

o an understanding of how the MDO came to be both a religious order and an order of ministry;
o an understanding by the Methodist Church of why the Order has always felt these two aspects of its life and work to be 'completely intertwined'
o a recognition that the nature and ministry of a renewed diaconate, including a renewed MDO, is intimately bound up with the nature and ministry of a renewed presbyterate.

o a realization that that the Resolutions concerned could have major implications, some detrimental, not only for the mission of Methodism but of the wider church.

5.2 Resolution 32/2

The Conference directs the Methodist Council, with the Methodist Diaconal Order and the Faith and Order Committee, to consider whether the religious order should be opened to receive into membership Methodists who are lay or ordained to presbyteral ministry and report to the 2018 Conference.

It can only be assumed that the reason for this Resolution is an assumption by the Faith and Order working party that lay people and presbyters are missing out on something which could be of great value to them if they were to become members of the MDO *as a religious order.* There is no doubt (as described earlier in this paper) that being a religious order bonds, energise and guides the MDO as an order of ministry. However, to invite laypeople and presbyters into membership of the MDO *as a religious order* and not an order of ministry would create many problems for the MDO, as well as for those coming into such a truncated form of 'membership' of the Order.

5.3 Problems for the MDO

As already stressed above, the MDO has for many years assumed that the two key facets of its life as an order of ministry and as a religious order are 'completely intertwined'. Although this 'intertwining' is not as yet enshrined in Methodist constitutional practice and discipline, it has for many years been implicit in the selection, training, ordination and practice of deacons. *The MDO does not exist only as a religious order.*

The Order is also committed to a distinctive apostolate which its life as a religious community nourishes, energises and guide. In the past, the Order's apostolate gained immensely from being nurtured and energised by its life as a religious community. If, in future, the apostolate of the MDO becomes that of facilitating the laity in a ministry of kingdom community building within society, as I advocate in this book, the Order's experience as a religious community would become even more important. Its life as a community would then exemplify and model the meaning of its community building apostolate.

5.4 Problems for presbyters and lay people

There would be major problems for presbyters and lay people who sought to join the MDO *only* as a religious order. These would include:

- o confusion as to which apostolate – presbyteral, lay or diaconal – their membership of the MDO as a religious order was related.
- o confusion as to their 'obligations' as set out in the Order's Rule of Life. For example should presbyters and lay people appear in the MDO's Daily Prayer Diary and should they be expected to attend area meetings of deacons and Convocation?

It is true that a very small number of those not deacons are currently designated as 'associates' of the MDO and their names appear in the Daily Prayer Diary. However, these are usually deacons who have become presbyters. They remain linked in this way simply because of a continuing interest in the Order to which they once belonged. They have no formal role or responsibilities in relation to the Order as such.

5.5 A way forward for presbyters

I believe that there is a far more constructive way forward for presbyters who feel strongly that they would benefit from becoming members of a religious order. It might be very beneficial for them to belong to *a presbyteral religious order*. Such a presbyteral order could well bond, nurture and energise presbyters in pursuit of their distinctive apostolate, not least if in future, this was one of an order of continuity enabling the gathered church to manifest the gifts of the kingdom community.

A religious order for presbyters could:

- o be adapted to support and develop a distinctive pesbyteral apostolate.
- o have a Rule of Life drawn up to reflect the nature and ethos of prebyteral ministry.
- o be sub-divided into regions, if large numbers opted to join it
- o have a 'Warden' of its own
- o keep closely in touch with the MDO through representation at the MDO's Convocation and perhaps occasional attendance at diaconal area meeting
- o be a matter of choice.

5.6 A way forward for lay people

There are already many opportunities for lay people to join religious communities of one kind or another – such as the Iona Community, the Corrymeela Community, the Northumbria Community, l'Arche and so on. What usually determines lay choice is the particular apostolate to which these communities are committed, a point which underlines what I have emphasised earlier in this paper about every religious order being formed around a distinctive apostolate.

Nevertheless, it is possible that there are lay people within Methodism who would wish to be more closely associated with the apostolate of the diaconal order or that of presbyteral ministry. In this case I believe that the best way forward would be that associated with the historic religious orders, such as the Franciscans who have a third order for lay people. Such a possible development is, in fact, hinted at in the Interim Report (5.4.7 (7)).

In fact, it might be supportive of deacons and presbyters developing new forms of apostolate, if Methodism were to initiate the formation of *two* such 'third Orders' of lay people. One lay order could be associated with the diaconate as an order of mission; the other with presbyters as an order of continuity. Each lay order could be seen as an integral part of the life and work of the orders of mission and continuity respectively, though less formally and fully involved than their ordained members. [See Paper 7 for the potential of a diaconal lay order.]

5.7 Resolution 33/3

> *The Conference directs the Methodist Council, with the Methodist Diaconal Order and the Faith and Order Committee, to consider whether those whom it ordains to the diaconal order of ministry continue to be required also to become members of the religious order and report to the 2018 Conference.*

As with Resolution 32/2, it is again unclear why the Faith and Order Committee's working party selected this as one of its only two Resolutions. Nor is it clear who would benefit from membership of the MDO as an order of ministry being split off from its life as a religious order. In practice, it would be a great loss to the MDO if this happened. Methodism would be turning its back on the precious heritage of the Wesley Deaconess Order and other Methodist diaconal associations. It would also be rejecting those features of is life as a religious order which empower and guide the apostolate of the MDO in the present, and need to do so in the future. *The MDO does not exist simply as an order of ministry.*

Those candidating for the MDO would find their ministry a good deal poorer if they were not required to accept the Order's Rule of Life. They would be deprived of that which powerfully bonds and enriches the life of deacons as a community. Of course, there are a few deacons who sit lightly to the Order's Rule of Life. However, they are far outweighed by the vast majority who treasure the latter. Those who candidate for the Order and are unaware of the degree to which its Rule of Life undergirds its life and work as a dispersed community, invariably come to appreciate the nature of the strong bonds such a Rule makes possible. As a presbyter who became a deacon, without initially recognizing the full significance of its Rule, I can personally bear witness to such an experience.

For some deacons to adhere to its Rule of Life and some to be excused from doing so would be divisive and confusing. As with Resolution 32/2, this situation would raise such issues as who was part of its collective prayer life, who should attend area groups and whether it was obligatory or not to attend Convocation. It would also raise the divisive question as to whether being a member of the MDO as an order of ministry was more important than being a member of the MDO as a religious order. A two-tier form of membership of the MDO is the last thing that would enhance the contribution of God's gift of a renewed diaconate to the mission of Methodism and the wider church.

May 2017

6 The 'new monasticism', the Methodist Diaconal Order and its calling as a new order of mission

Preamble

Throughout the history of the Christian church, there have been those that have felt called to live out their faith in ways that exemplify what it means to be a Christian community. From early monasticism to the Christian community movement of the late twentieth century, this has usually been done 'on the edges' of society, a fact that has sometimes raised the question of the relevance of such witness for those living in the maelstrom of urban life. However, the relevance for the church to come of attempts to model what these papers call the nature and form of the kingdom community are important initiatives and need careful consideration. The purpose of this paper is to explore the meaning and potential of the so-called 'new monasticism' and to evaluate its relevance to the future of the Methodist Diaconal Order and the wider church.

1 Introduction

The term 'new monasticism' is that given to a diverse range of 'intentional communities' of all faiths that have sprung up across the world in recent years. They have emerged in many countries. However, their development has been particularly evident in the USA. This paper is concerned with the new monasticism as a Christian phenomenon and how it relates to the *British* scene.[1]

Most groups on the British scene associated with the new monasticism have a very limited number of features which reflect pre-Reformation monastic communities. For example, the NMCs do not take vows which are life-long. Most ask their members to commit themselves to the community for one or two years only, after which they are free to go their several ways. Members of NMCs do not take traditional vows of poverty, celibacy and obedience. Married couples are sometimes members of the community.

---

[1] For ease of reading, I abbreviate the term 'new monastic community' to NMC.

There is no strict obedience to a leader, as was the case with the abbot or prior in pre-Reformation times. Many NMCs do not require their members to live together in one dwelling and consequently take the form of dispersed rather than gathered communities. Most British NMCs would thus appear to be more akin to 'intentional communities', groups making an informal commitment to live together as, or associate with, some form of core community.

Nor are many groups currently referred to as NMCs very 'new'. In Britain, only a dozen or so have appeared since the turn of the century. Most other so-called 'NMCs' were in fact up set up from the late 1930s onwards, of which the Iona Community is probably the most well-known.

1.1 The late twentieth century Christian Community Movement

Between the two world wars, a number of communities, intentional and otherwise, sprung up, notably to witness for peace and non-violence. In the post second world war period, many were committed to a ministry of reconciliation (Focolare, Othona, Taizé). However, from the 1960s there was a veritable explosion of such communities. Their apostolates were, amongst other issues, related to peace and justice (Corrymeela, Roadrunners); human welfare (l'Arche, Bystock Court, the Cyrenians, Pilsdon, Sheffield Ashram); the environment (Ringsfield Hall, Scoraig); life-style (Blackheath Commune, Laurieston Hall, Lothlorien); and spirituality (The Grail, Taena) (Clark, 1977).

So prolific was the growth of Christian communities and groups in the 1970s and 1980s[1] that, in 1980, a National Centre for Christian Communities and Networks (NACCCAN) was established in Birmingham. It was foreshadowed by a magazine entitled *Community*, which I began in 1970 and was published for 30 years. The National Centre was also preceded, in 1977, by a unique gathering of recently formed Christian communities and groups, together with representatives of the Anglican and Roman Catholic religious orders, which met at Hengrave Hall in Suffolk.

---

[1] A number of my books document the Christian community movement of this period. Four of particularly note are: Clark (1977) *Basic* Communities; (1984) *The Liberation of the Church*; (1987) *Yes to Life*; and (2005) *Breaking the Mould of Christendom*.

In 1980, the first of three national congresses, which brought together members of the Christian Community Movement, was held in Birmingham. Representatives of 106 Christian groups and intentional communities, and of 42 religious orders (13 Anglican and 29 Roman Catholic) attended. The congress was addressed by three leading figures of the movement: Jean Vanier (l'Arche), Rosemary Haughton (Lothlorien) and Jim Wallis (Sojourners, USA). A *Directory* published for the congress listed some 250 Christian groups, communities and networks and 200 religious orders. Two further national congresses were held, in 1984 and 1987.

It is not the intention of this paper to survey the complex reasons for the decline, after the 1980s, of this dynamic community movement as this has been done elsewhere (Clark, 2005, pp. 159-169). However, where relevant to the life and work of contemporary NMCs, some of these reasons will be touched on below.

2 New monastic communities

2.1 Features of the New Monastic Communities

Although the NMCs are in most respects neither monastic nor new, they do have important features typical of many intentional Christian communities. Their apostolate is often of a contemplative nature with prayer, personal and collective, as central. Most have a rule of life. They agree to follow a rhythm of prayer, worship and meeting together during the week. Their apostolate is often linked to offering hospitality alongside a commitment to serve the marginalized and disadvantaged. The members often live together in a community house and accept responsibility for its upkeep. Most communities have a 'head' or warden of some kind. One or two have a 'habit' which they wear mainly on public occasions.

2.2 The contribution of the new monastic communities to church and society

The NMCs make a helpful contribution to the life of the institutional church. They engage a number of younger people in a way of life which can enrich their understanding of and strengthen their commitment to the Christian faith. They help to remind the wider church of its great heritage of spirituality and prayer. Many strive to model a collective pattern of leadership. They witness to the essential place that caring for those on the margins of society should have in the mission of the church. Thus, through their life and their apostolates, NMCs offer helpful insights for church and world into what it means to be a Christian community in this day and age.

In other respects, the contribution of NMCs to the church present is more limited. Even if all those communities currently associated with the new monastic movement (well-established or recent) are included, their overall numbers remain tiny compared with the lay resources of the church as a whole. Their life as Christian communities does not naturally reflect the life-style of the traditional gathered church and thus their modelling of community can seem to regular church members somewhat 'artificial'. Their apostolate as a community is not one that lay people in employment usually have the inclination or time to replicate. The relatively short-term commitment to their community does not really test out the latter's staying power.

Many NMCs appear to be closely tied to the institutional church. For example, the Hollywell Community in Abergavenny, the Way2Community in Truro, the Community of St Margaret the Queen in Streatham, the Community of St Anselm at Lambeth, and the recently formed Wellspring Community in Peckham (*Church Times*, 2/6/17), rely a good deal on clerical instigation and diocesan support, financial and otherwise.

3 The new monastic communities and the Methodist Diaconal Order

3.1 Comparison of the MDO and NMCs urged

The Methodist Diaconal Order (MDO), springing out of the long history of the Wesley Deaconess Order, came into being in 1986. It was then opened to women and men. In 1993 the Methodist Conference affirmed the MDO as being a religious order, thus acknowledging its historic continuity with the Wesley Deaconess Order.

In 1998, all deacons were received into 'Full Connexion', as far as church order was concerned, putting deacons on an equal footing with presbyters. In 2004, the Methodist Conference approved the report *What is a Deacon?* as an authoritative description of the life and work of the MDO. By 2018, there were nearly 140 active members of the Order.

In May 2016, a working party of Methodism's Faith and Order Committee, set up by the Methodist Conference to explore the theology and ecclesiology underpinning the MDO, published its Interim Report. This states (5.4.7):

> While recruitment to traditional religious orders has declined sharply – at least in the West – there has in recent years been an upsurge in what has been called 'new monasticism'. These groups, many of which include Methodists in their membership, deserve fuller attention. They may well suggest ways in which the MDO could develop in the future and they might also help the MDO express what is particular about its own style of religious order.

As noted, the term 'upsurge' is something of an exaggeration. For example, of the six 'NMCs' mentioned in the Interim Report, only one (the St Anselm Community) was founded in the last thirty years. Nevertheless, as the report suggests, it is still important to consider what NMCs might have to offer to the life and work of the Methodist Diaconal Order and the wider church.

3.1.1 Communal life

As religious communities, the NMCs and the MDO have a number of features in common. They both reflect some of the hall-marks of traditional religious communities, pre-eminent among which is a rule of life to which all members are pledged. This rule embraces the development of a personal and communal spiritualty and mutual pastoral support. Though the MDO is far more dispersed than the members of most NMCs, deacons meet and pray regularly in small area groups.

However, differences between NMCs and the MDO clearly exist. NMCs espouse a more regular, face-to-face and 'intense' form of worship and prayer, often with a recurring weekly rhythm shaping it. This is not possible for Methodist deacons who are widely scattered across the country. Most NMCs possess a community house to which they relate in a symbolic and personal way. This offers a strong focal point for the meeting, worship and mutual support of members and associates. The MDO possessed its own 'mother house' until very recently but now has only a room in Methodist Church House, London, albeit well designed and attractively set out, as a home base.

In past years, the MDO, and the Wesley Deaconess Order before it, set up a number of community houses, with several deacons in residence, in order to address the needs of the local area. Not many such houses lasted very long. Consequently it is possible that the MDO might learn something from NMCs about the challenges facing any intentional community and how to respond to these. However, it is just as likely that lessons could be learnt from intentional communities which have been in existence for many decades, such as l'Arche or Corrymeela, or from those historic religious orders which are still relatively strong, such as the Anglican or Roman Catholic Franciscans.

Most recently founded NMCs, as well as the MDO, are linked closely to the particular denomination which helped to bring them into being. However, a number of older communities – such as Iona (1938), Othona (1946), Corrymeela (1964) and l'Arche (1964) – and some more recent ones – such as the Northumbria Community (1980s) – exist more on the edges of the mainstream denominations. This offers them greater freedom to explore alternatives to a now anachronistic Christendom model of the church. However, awareness of and contributing to a diaconal model of church, as described in these papers, is not on the agenda of more recently formed NMCs.

3.1.2 *Their apostolates*

Both the NMCs and the MDO in principle espouse an apostolate which places the needs of the marginalized and poor at the forefront of their ministries.

However, because members of NMCs are usually in full-time employment, their time has inevitably to be shared between their workplace and any initiatives which the NMC undertakes. Methodist deacons are ordained and committed full-time to what the church requires of them. In principle this means responding to the needs of the marginalized. However, because their work is very much tied to the immediate requirements of the circuit and/or gathered churches where they are 'stationed', their responsibilities may not immediately be concerned with the needs of those on the edges of society.

In contrast to NMCs and the MDO today, the Christian community movement of the 1960s and 1970s spawned many groups and communities committed to giving their whole attention to modelling an 'alternative' society and world (Clark, 1977 and 1984). Their apostolates were not only about a new approach to spirituality, but related to justice and peace issues, environmental and economic concerns, educational matters, issues of health and healing, penal reform or innovative social welfare developments, amongst other things. However, their endeavours remained most impressive as human scale prototypes of what might be achieved than transformational at a societal level and in an enduring sense. This was a fundamental limitation which I address below.

4 The continuing neglect of the laity

The Interim Report of the Faith and Order working party of the Methodist Church suggests that the MDO might look at the life and work of NMCs to see what could be learnt from them. As argued above, my own conviction is that more could be learnt from the Christian community movement of the 1970s and 1980s and the challenges it faced in relation to church *and* society. This is not to devalue the life and work of NMCs. It is simply to argue that they appear to be more about continuity than transformation. Thus they do not offer any particularly fresh models of religious life or awareness of what a Christian apostolate in a post-Christendom age should look like.

However, neither the NMCs nor the MDO have, as yet, seriously addressed the gaping 'hole' in the mission resources of the church in the twenty-first century. That 'hole' is what Mark Gibbs and Ralph Morton many years ago called *God's Frozen People* (1964). What Gibbs and Morton were describing was the inability of the church to educate and equip its laity (a resource far surpassing the membership of all NMCs and the MDO taken together) for a mission which would help transform the secular institutions of society into kingdom collectives (Clark, 2005).

To fill this 'hole' by 'unfreezing' the people of God, two radical developments are needed, which I have addressed in other papers in this book. However, I repeat them here. First and foremost, is working out a kingdom theology of mission in which the transformation of society and not the survival of church is at the top of the agenda.

The second development is bringing into being a new form of Christian leadership. It would be concerned with raising the awareness of lay people to the need for all the major sectors of a secular society to manifest more fully the hall-marks of the kingdom community – life, liberation, love and learning. Such leadership would also be concerned with educating and equipping lay people for the task of making that vision a reality. It is a development which would necessitate the training of Christian leaders with the imagination, skills and commitment to undertake, amongst other roles, that of mentor (Clark, 2014).

It is my contention that Methodism and the wider church should cease promoting a host of ad hoc leadership roles with ambiguous and even divisive titles such as 'pioneer ministers'. Instead, the Methodist Church should train and give authority to what would become a new diaconal order of mission called to equip the people of God to exercise their ministry as the church in the world. In doing so I believe Methodism would be responding to what many worldwide are discerning as God's gift of a renewed diaconate to the church to come.

June 2017

7 The case for a Methodist diaconal lay order

Preamble

The suggestion that the Methodist Church should consider bringing into being a lay (often called 'third') order, as a distinct entity or as an integral part of the Methodist Diaconal Order, is not new. In March 2007, the Interim Report of the Stationing Review Group proposed that diaconal ministry might be opened to lay people without them being required to join the Methodist Diaconal Order, or, alternatively, that membership of the Methodist Diaconal Order might be opened to lay people. However, in 2008, the Review Group's final report to the Methodist Conference concluded that this proposal had, at least for the moment, been 'a step too far' (R3, 3-5).

In 2016, the Interim Report of the Faith and Order Committee, a group commissioned to undertake an exploration of *The Theology and Ecclesiology underpinning the Diaconate*, which was presented to the Methodist Conference of that year, recommended that the latter direct 'the Methodist Council, with the Methodist Diaconal Order and the Faith and Order Committee, to consider whether the (Methodist Diaconal Order as a) religious order should be opened to receive into membership Methodists who are lay… ' (33/2). However, the reason for this resolution was not clearly explained by material set out in the body of the report in which there was only one fleeting reference to the concept of a 'third order' (5.4.7 (7)).

This paper has been prompted by the initiatives mentioned above and by conversations set up by a Methodist Council working party (its work apparently completed but its findings not yet known). These conversations, attended by some fifty Methodist deacons, were held at the Queens College, Birmingham at the end of 2017, when the potential of a lay 'third order' associated with the MDO was one item on the agenda.

1 What is a 'third order'?

1.1 Origins

Historically, a 'third order' is an association of persons who have committed themselves to live according to the ideals and spirit of a Roman Catholic, Anglican or Lutheran religious order, but who do not belong to a 'first order' (generally, in the Catholic Church, of male religious) or a 'second order' (of female religious associated with the 'first order'). Members of third orders are known as 'tertiaries' (from the Latin for 'third'). They are usually lay men or women, and sometimes those who are ordained, who do not take religious vows as such but participate in the 'charism' (good works) of the order. If they live together, they are sometimes known as 'regulars'; if they live as individuals in the world, as 'seculars'.

Lay people, such as Benedictine Oblates, were affiliated to religious orders early in the life of the church. However, the emergence of associations of tertiaries is seen as an innovation of the thirteenth century. It is almost certain that the lead was taken by the Franciscans. The Franciscan Third Order, approved by the Pope in 1221, was the exemplar after which many others third orders, such as that associated with the Dominicans, were modelled.

The Second Vatican Council (1962-1965) gave great prominence to the concept of lay vocation and the sanctification of family life, daily life and all secular occupations. Consequently, many new lay Catholic voluntary associations appeared. At the same time, the concept of 'tertiary' was deepened and broadened to stress that this meant the living out of the lay Christian vocation within secular life in the spirit of the order with which the lay person was associated.

2 A lay third order and two dispersed lay communities

Before presenting the case for Methodism to explore the creation of a lay (third) order associated with the Methodist Diaconal Order (henceforth called the MDO), it is helpful to look at the nature of three contemporary lay communities which might offer insights into characteristics which help focus and sustain this form of association: the Third Order of the Anglican Order of St Francis, the Iona Community and the Northumbria Community.

One reason for choosing these examples is that they are all *dispersed* lay communities. Though their members are committed to an apostolate (or calling) which reflects the vocation of the whole community, individuals are widely scattered and only come together occasionally in local groups or at their 'mother house'. The MDO is likewise a widely dispersed community. So would be any lay order associated with it.

Many lay communities, for example l'Arche which works with those with learning difficulties, encourage 'volunteers' to offer their services to further their particular 'apostolates' (the specific work to which they feel called). However, they are not necessarily dispersed communities, nor would all of them have 'degrees of association' for those wanting to commit themselves to the community's apostolate. However, two lay communities which are dispersed and do have degrees of association are the Iona Community and the more recently formed Northumbria Community. Their life and work will be considered a little later.

2.1 The Third Order of the Anglican Order of the Society of St. Francis

The religious order which perhaps reflects the nature and ethos of the MDO most closely, and thus which might offer guidance as to the nature of a Methodist lay (third) order, is the Anglican Order of the Society of St. Francis.[1] This was founded in 1950 and consists of men and women, lay and ordained, married and single. It now has some 3000 members and consists of five provinces: Europe, Africa, Australia, New Zealand and the Americas. The mother house of the European Province is at Hilfield in Dorset.

Third Order Anglican Franciscans espouse no specific ministry or apostolate. Members exercise different ministries according to the gifts that God has given them. However, the Anglican Third Order is founded on three Principles. These are:

'To make our Lord known and loved everywhere...
To spread the spirit of love and harmony -
  The Order sets out, in the name of Christ, to break down barriers between people and to seek equality for all...
To live simply -

---

[1] For more information about the Franciscan Third Order see: www.tssf.org.uk

> Although we possess property and earn money to support
> ourselves and our families, we show ourselves true followers of
> Christ and of St. Francis by our readiness to live simply and to
> share with others...'

These Principles are expressed through a Personal Rule of Life
which, in its practical application, is adapted to the circumstances of
each tertiary.

Those applying to join the 'Fraternity' of Franciscan tertiaries are
required to pass through the stages of being an enquirer, a postulant (for
about six months) and a novice (for at least two years), before becoming
a professed member of the third order.

2.1.1 What have the Franciscans to offer to the MDO and any associated lay order?

The Franciscan Order as a whole is dedicated to following in the
footsteps of St Francis with his commitment to poverty and a ministry
to the poor. It is an apostolate which echoes that of Methodism and
the MDO (and Wesley Deaconess Order before the MDO came into
being) in their historical concern for the poor and marginalized within
society.

Franciscans feel a particular call to holiness and the quest for
Christian perfection. Similarly, Methodism has at its heart the search
for holiness. I have elsewhere called this 'communal holiness' [see
Appendix].

Respect for life in all its forms, human and otherwise, is high on the
Franciscan agenda, an approach which reflects Methodism's concern for
the future of the planet.

The Rule of the Franciscan Third Order has a good deal in common
with that of the MDO. It includes a commitment to study, to meet in
local groups, to make a retreat each year and to an annual renewal of
promises. Thus it is likely that any Rule for a lay order associated with
the MDO would reflect the latter's Rule.

As well as in other ways, the Franciscan Third Order is bonded by
being able to meet from time to time at the Order's mother house in
Hilfield.

2.2 The Iona Community

The Iona Community was founded in Glasgow and Iona in 1938 by George MacLeod, minister, visionary and prophetic witness for peace, in the context of the poverty and despair of the mid-war economic depression.[1] From a dockland parish in Govan, Glasgow, he took unemployed skilled craftsmen and young trainee clergy to the island of Iona to rebuild the monastic quarters of the mediaeval abbey. In the process they shared a common life working and living together. The original task of renovating the abbey was the impetus for an ongoing commitment to rebuild community life in Scotland and beyond, with an emphasis on the pursuit of justice and peace. The experience shaped – and continues to shape – the practice and principles of the Iona Community.

Members of the Iona Community commit themselves to a Rule as follows:

> 'Daily prayer, worship with others and regular engagement with the Bible and other material which nourishes us.
> Working for justice and peace, wholeness and reconciliation in our localities, society and the whole creation.
> Supporting one another in prayer and meeting, communicating, and accounting with one another for the use of our gifts, money and time, our use of the earth's resources and our keeping of all aspects of the Rule.
> Sharing in the corporate life and organization of the Community.'

This Rule is developed further in a list of beliefs, working principles, values (environmental, social and economic) and commitments. The life and work of the Community are based on transparency, democratic decision making and mutual accountability. As a dispersed community, Members are required to meet regularly throughout the year in local groups and in plenary gatherings, including a week spent on Iona. They are asked to give a written undertaking annually that they are 'with the Community' in their commitment to its Rule.

Associates are required to affirm their agreement with the Community's concerns and work. They are invited to keep the Rule

---

[1] For more information about the Iona Community see: www.*iona.org.uk*

as far as they are able. They are offered the opportunity to meet with other Members and Associates in regional groups. After two years as an Associate, they can opt to become Members of the Community.

The Iona Community also offers the informal status of Friends, who support its life and work in diverse ways, including financially, and of Volunteers, who offer practical help whenever they can.

2.2.1 What has the Iona Community to offer to the MDO and any associated lay order?

The Iona Community is an association in its own right. However, its Rule not only reflects that of the MDO, but could help to inform a lay order linked to the latter.

The Iona Community's apostolate is particularly concerned about issues of justice and peace. This is very much in tune with the Windsor Statement published by an ecumenical group of deacons, including members of the MDO, in 1997. This includes the words:

> Opening doors of opportunity; encouraging others to take risks; the contemporary diaconate acting in its capacity as 'agent of change'; engages imaginatively and collaboratively with issues of justice, poverty, social and environmental concerns.

The requirements for full membership of the Iona Community have many features from which a lay order associated with the MDO would benefit.

As a widely dispersed association, the Iona Community gains an immense amount through having a church and a 'mother house' on the island of Iona, enriched by the latter's history of Christian mission. The mother house and church are available for worship and many other kinds of gathering.

2.3 The Northumbria Community

The Northumbria Community[1] describes itself as 'a diverse and dispersed network of people, alone and together, gathered around a Rule of Life as *a* Way to follow *the* Way'. It believes that it has been 'brought

---

[1] For more information about the Northumbria Community see: www.northumbria community.org

into existence as a Community to call people back to a relational God, seeking Him daily, as the one thing necessary, in the cell of our own hearts'. It states that 'as Companions in Community, we are united in our desire to embrace and express an ongoing exploration into a new way for living, through a new monasticism, as Christians, that offers hope in our changed and changing culture.'

The Northumbria Community has a somewhat complex history. In 1992, Hatton Hall in Northumberland became the mother house for an emerging community, the origins of which go back to certain individual visionary initiatives of the previous decade. Its daily office, *Celtic Daily Prayer*, was published in 1994, when the group officially adopted the name Northumbria Community. During the 1990s' numbers grew and related groups were established in Europe. In 2010, the Community changed its base to Acton Home Farm, Northumbria where it is currently situated (called Nether Springs and being known as 'the mother house'). More recent years have seen the Community increasing steadily in size and going international, with Community groups in Europe, Canada, the USA and Australia.

The Community has two categories of associate: Companions and Friends. The term 'Companion' is more than nominal and means 'a person who associates with another, shares their life style and travels with them'. The term 'Friend' is more informal and refers to anyone who supports the work of the Community through interest, prayer and financial help.

The process of becoming a Companion has three stages: being a postulant, and attending 'a Community introduction retreat'; next being a novitiate, with accompanied distance learning focused on the Rule of the Community for about a year, regular use of the Daily Office, a week spent as a volunteer at the mother house and some form of retreat; then being a Companion, including a public welcome into the Community.

The Community places its Rule of Life at the heart of the life of Companions. The Rule has two foci stated as: 'We are called to be AVAILABLE to God and to others' and 'We are called to intentional, deliberate VULNERABILITY'. The former emphasises the need for being inwardly available to God and outwardly available to meet the needs of the world. The latter emphasises the need to be 'teachable', but also prepared to challenge the status quo and live 'as a community of the heart' and 'a church without walls'.

Amongst other things, a Companion is committed to reflect annually with another Companion on their spiritual journey, use the Community Prayer Guide, make an annual renewal of 'vows', attend a Community area group, support the mother house and make a financial contribution to the Community.

The Community comes together in Community Groups which include Friends and other interested persons, and Community Gatherings which share fellowship, learning and meals for a day. Community Teams, termed 'a monastery on the road... go to churches, other communities..., festivals, conferences, workplaces, schools..., hospitals, etc.' to communicate the nature and work of the Community.

2.3.1 What has the Northumbria Community to offer to the MDO and any associated lay order?

The MDO and any associated lay order could learn from the fact that the primary feature of the Northumbria Community is its commitment to offering a new and dynamic spirituality for lay people, meaningful and sustainable in the hectic life of a secular society. The Community's Rule of Life is all-important and great care is taken to keep the meaning and expression of this fresh and relevant to daily life.

The Rule is seen as shaping a shared journey of spiritual discovery by persons engaged in what is described as 'a community of the heart'. The Northumbria Community is pre-eminently a learning community, a feature which should also permeate the life of the MDO and any associated lay order.

Becoming a Companion of the Community is regarded as a serious step. This is why the Community sees strong relationships between, and the support of other Companions and Friends as essential.

The Community stresses the centrality of the cell, which it believes may well form the foundation of a future 'church without walls'.

As 'a dispersed network', the Northumbria Community regards its mother house, Nether Springs, as a vital symbolic and practical communal resource. In this context, and a similar situation existing for the Franciscan Third Order and the Iona Community, it would seem worthwhile for the Methodist Church to review whether it was wise to have closed the MDO's 'mother house' in Birmingham and look for another way of providing a genuinely communal 'home' for the MDO.

3 Hall-marks of Methodism which open the way to the creation of a diaconal lay order

In many respects Methodism first emerged as a form of lay order from within the Church of England of its day. However, because the latter failed to affirm this development, Methodism was obliged to branch out on its own. Over time Methodism followed the normative sociological pattern of developing from a sect (or society) into a denomination, and then into an institution. Nevertheless, in the process, it has retained two characteristics which make it a church well suited to encompass a religious order and a lay order closely associated with the latter. These characteristics are: the primacy Methodism gives to the pursuit of holiness, and the pre-eminent place of the laity in that undertaking. The former feature is reflected in the existence of the Methodist Diaconal Order as a religious order, a situation affirmed by the Methodist Conference in 1993. The creation of an associated lay order would enhance the latter characteristic.

3.1 The pursuit of 'communal holiness'

Methodism has always been a church which places the concept of *koinonia*, or community, at its heart. No Conference report reflects this fact more eloquently than *Called to Love and Praise,* one of the most important statements on the life of Methodism as a church produced in recent years. This report stresses again and again 'the essential nature of the Church as *koinonia*', seen as 'both a gift and a calling' (3.1.6 and 3.1.7). That calling is the pursuit of holiness, or perfect love, but as a social not solitary undertaking (4.2.14; 4.3.8; 4.3.9). Consequently, I have argued elsewhere that the fundamental calling of Methodism is to further 'communal holiness' within its own life and that of society [see Appendix]. To this end, the Methodist Church is required to offer the world examples of communal holiness in practice. The Methodist Diaconal Order is one such example. So could be a new diaconal lay order.

3.2 The primacy of the laity

Methodism believes that 'the ministry of the people of God in the world is both the primary and normative ministry of the Church' (1988; 1990, 4.5.4). However, two factors in particular have negated this conviction. One is the development of clericalism within Methodism. This has led to a church seen as pre-dominantly led and represented by its ordained ministry not its laity. The other factor, and in large part a consequence of clericalism, is the increasingly inward focus of lay ministry which has come to be regarded as about the maintenance of the church not the transformation of society. The creation of a diaconal lay order could help to re-affirm the primacy of 'the ministry of the people of God in the world'.

4 The nature of a Methodist diaconal lay order

4.1 Its apostolate – builders of kingdom communities

All religious orders and their associated third orders, as well as lay communities such as the Iona Community and Northumbria Community, embrace a distinctive apostolate (a calling) which shapes their life and work. It is this apostolate which initially draws people towards the order or community concerned, gives it a sense of purpose, direction and impetus, and bonds its members together. This paper contends that the apostolate of a lay order within Methodism should reflect the apostolate of the Methodist Diaconal Order. It would thus be a *diaconal* lay order.

In a number of papers preceding this one[1], I have argued that the church of the future will be a diaconal, or servant church. It will be the servant of what I call 'the kingdom community', the latter offering the world a glimpse of the meaning of communal holiness at its zenith, including a deep concern for the well-being of the disadvantaged and marginalized. I have also argued that Methodism embraces many features of a diaconal church, not least in its pursuit of communal holiness and the primacy it seeks to give to its laity in that task [see Appendix].

Within the diaconal church, the apostolate of the people of God in the world is to become kingdom community builders wherever they live,

---

[1] See especially Paper 1

work or play. Thus the apostolate of God's gift of a renewed diaconate, including of a renewed Methodist Diaconal Order, needs to move away from its historic focus on 'witness through service' to become that of equipping lay people for their task of kingdom community building in daily life. A renewed diaconate will be the diaconal church's mission enablers.

Members of a new lay order would reflect this distinctive diaconal calling. They would exemplify in their own life and work, and help the whole church to comprehend what it means to be kingdom community builders, that is, creators of communal holiness.

4.2 Its spiritual life as a lay order

The spirituality of a diaconal lay order would be greatly enriched and deepened by its being an integral part of the life and work of the MDO as a religious order. To further this development, the MDO's Rule of Life could become a basis for the new lay order (see section 6).

5 Benefits of the creation of a Methodist diaconal lay order

5.1 What would be the benefits for those called into such a lay order?

o They would become models for the mission of the people of God in the world.

o They would gain a sense of significance by helping to pioneer a new vision of the mission of the church in the world.

o They would be given the incentive to equip themselves more fully as kingdom community builders through prayer, study, discussion and reflective practice.

o Their life and work would be empowered through an enriched communal spirituality.

o They would experience a powerful sense of belonging to their colleagues in such a third order and to deacons in the Methodist Diaconal Order.

5.2 What would be the benefits for the Methodist Diaconal Order?

o A diaconal lay order would offer Methodist deacons fresh and informative models of how to engage in ministry and mission in daily life, not least the world of work.

o It would offer the MDO the expertise and resources of many of those still actively engaged in the life of society.

o A new lay order would offer deacons greater opportunity for colleagueship from a network, similar to itself, dispersed across the country.

o It would encourage deacons to review how well they are living out their own Rule of Life and fulfilling their own apostolate.

5.3 What would be the benefits for Methodism and the wider church?

o A diaconal lay order would inform and inspire Methodism and the wider church as to what it means to be an order of mission in today's world.

o Methodism and the wider church would be enlightened and enthused by examples of what the ministry of the laity could mean in a post Christendom age.

o Methodism and the wider church would get a clearer understanding of the meaning of the diaconal calling as that of kingdom community building.

o Methodism would gain a greater awareness and appreciation of the contribution of the Methodist Diaconal Order and an associated lay order to the renewal of the permanent diaconate within all churches

6 How the MDO's Rule of Life might be reflected in a Rule of Life for a diaconal lay order

The MDO's Rule of Life is set out below. I believe that, amended as indicated by the deletions and words added in italics, this might offer a basis for the creation of a Rule of Life for a diaconal lay order. A similar form for the MDO's and a lay order's Rule of Life would have the advantage of linking the two orders closely in commitment and ethos.

Devotional life

We endeavour to:

- attend worship regularly, especially Holy Communion
- set aside time each day to read the Bible devotionally and to pray, including a time of intercession for members of the *MDO and lay order*
- regularly set aside time for self-examination ~~= a chance to look back and see where we have failed in loving God and our neighbours and to give thanks for blessings received~~
- ~~find a spiritual director/Companion, who will accompany, help and affirm us~~
- ~~make time each year for a retreat or quiet day.~~

Discipline

We endeavour to:

- be sensitive to the needs of ~~those close to us,~~ our families, dependents, and friends *and work colleagues*
- ~~be aware of and relate to, the community in which we live~~ *strive for the coming of the kingdom in neighbourhood, workplace and society*
- acknowledge and enjoy God's gifts to us of time, talents, money and possessions and through God's grace be able stewards of these
- order the rhythm of each day, month and year, to allow for study and relaxation ~~and holidays~~
- attend an annual *diaconal lay order Assembly (possibly held during Convocation)* ~~(unless a dispensation is granted)~~
- *together with members of the MDO,* participate in the life of area groups ~~wherever possible and attend meetings~~
- keep in contact with *and support* other members of the lay order. ~~by giving or receiving of fellowship and support, by visits, letter or telephone.~~

7 What practical issues would be associated with this development?

7.1 Names

I have argued in this paper that the name of a new order associated with the MDO should be the 'Methodist diaconal lay order'. I would suggest that members of the new order should be known not as tertiaries, but as 'Companions'. This not only has a more contemporary ring about it but would emphasise the communal nature of the order.

7.2 Numbers

It is impossible at this stage to estimate how many lay people would join such an order. However, if it were affirmed by Conference and promoted across the Connexion, membership could well grow to fifty, and if welcomed as a 'fresh expression of church', perhaps more.

7.3 Selection, preparation, reception and beyond

As with the Anglican Franciscan Third Order, those wishing to join the new order would need to demonstrate their commitment to the order's apostolate and Rule of Life. Thus some process of selection of possible members of the order would need to be put into place.

Potential Companions would be expected to test out their calling over an appropriate period of time before being received into the lay order. Reception into membership could take place at an annual Assembly of the lay order, or possibly at the MDO's Convocation in order to stress the bond between the two orders. This bond could also be strengthened by Companions being presented with the badge of the MDO.

7.4 Living by a Rule of Life

Companions would be bonded and guided by a shared Rule of Life. If numbers permitted, praying for fellow Companions might be extended to praying for members of the MDO, aided by the provision of a more comprehensive prayer handbook which included members of both orders.

7.5 Keeping in touch

Companions would be encouraged to attend area groups set up for deacons. This would help to make some area groups, where deacons are thin on the ground, more viable.

The annual Assembly of the lay order would be a key gathering and could take the form of a free-standing event or, in some way, be linked to Convocation. Companions would be urged to attend the MDO's Convocation (though having no vote), perhaps on a particular day when the agenda would facilitate attention to the lay order's life and work and its relationship with the MDO.

The lay order would need some form of regular 'order paper' which might be linked to that of the MDO.

7.6 Finance

Financially, members of a new lay order would usually have a self-supporting ministry.

8 Implications for Methodism

8.1 A diaconal lay order's place within the Connexion

To have standing in the life of the Connexion, a new lay order would need recognition by the Methodist Conference. The former's structures, procedures and membership would need identifying, approval and recording in the same way as those of the MDO.

It would be crucial that the reasons for launching such an order were communicated to the Connexion, especially to local churches which at the moment are sometimes confused as to the role and responsibilities of the MDO.

Getting such an order in place is likely to take some time, with inevitably small beginnings. The Connexion would need to be committed to at least a five year development strategy.

8.2 Oversight

A new lay order would require oversight. It is likely that the order would need its own lay 'Warden', self-supporting or paid, who would work very closely with the leadership of the MDO.

8.3 A new centre

If such an order came into being, the Connexion should look again at the creation of a new 'mother house' to be used by both the lay order and the MDO. The examples of the Franciscans, with the mother house in Dorset, as well as the Iona Community and the Northumbria Community, underline the importance of having such a centre.

9 Some questions

9.1 Would such an order call into question the status of those who are already designated as 'Associates' and 'Friends' of the MDO?

No. The current 'Associate' deacon category (originally known as 'Friends') is an informal in-house designation and has no authorized status as far as the Methodist Conference is concerned. There do not appear to be any agreed guidelines for the nomination or responsibilities of the few current Associates. In 2018 there were 27 Associates of the MDO.

The 'Associate' category was originally designed to let those who changed their order from deaconess/sister or deacon to presbyter, to retain a personal link with the MDO. Historically, this applied to those who moved into presbyteral ministry when it became possible for women to candidate for that order. However, others who have changed orders in more recent years have usually declined Associate status. At the same time, some Wardens granted Associate status to a small number of individuals, lay or ordained, because it was felt that they had contributed significantly to the work of the order.

Likewise, the current category of 'Friend' is informal in character. It appears simply to indicate those on the MDO's mailing list who have contributed, mainly financially, to its life or work.

9.2 Would a new diaconal lay order be too small and scattered to make any significant contribution to the MDO, Methodism or the wider church?

The benchmark by which to measure the value of a new lay order is its quality not its quantity. All new movements in the life of the church have begun with a handful of people with a vision and a commitment to make that vision a reality. The creation of a new diaconal lay order would in itself be a visionary initiative which could enrich the life of the church to come, not least in giving impetus and support to the development of the MDO and other diaconal associations as orders of mission. (Clark, 2016)

9.3 Is there a danger that such an order would be dominantly made up of retired people with time on their hands?

A key aspect of the apostolate of a diaconal lay order is to help give new meaning and impetus to the ministry and mission of the people of God in the world. This means that those selected for such an order need to be actively engaged in the life and work of a secular society. If they are retired, and many lay people exercise an inspiring ministry in retirement, Companions of such an order should still be able to demonstrate that they are concerned about and actively involved in organisations addressing key issues of contemporary life.

9.4 Can such an order be financed?

The intention is that a new lay order would attract people who are currently earning a salary or have a pension which can support themselves and their families. They would commit themselves to become Companions of such an order whilst continuing to be actively engaged in their daily work or, as retired, in voluntary endeavours. It is the expression of their faith through their life and work, paid or voluntary, not the offering of their time to maintain the institutional church, that is the hall-mark of their being Companions of the order.

9.5 Would members of a lay order have to be itinerant?

No. They would exercise their ministry where they live and where they work.

9.6 Is it necessary to link the term 'diaconal' to such a lay order?

This question goes to the heart of the theology and ecclesiology on which this and the other papers in this book are based. The papers are founded on a theology which takes the coming of the kingdom, now and in the future, as that which gives meaning to ministry and mission in today's world. They are also founded on the conviction that because the church is first and foremost the servant of that kingdom, it is a diaconal, or servant church. Thus any order which is an integral part of a church which seeks to be the servant of the kingdom is a diaconal order.

It is the contention of this and other papers that the office of deacon should, in this day and age, be that of enabling lay people to be servants of the kingdom, wherever they live, work of play. Attaching the word 'diaconal' to a new lay order is to stress that Companions remain 'commissioned' representatives of, and models for the servant ministry of the whole people of God in the world.

9.7 Is there a danger that the creation of a lay order will be regarded as élitist?

This depends on the nature of the order's apostolate and the role it seeks to play in fulfilling it. Few would call Third Order Franciscans, with their concern to help the marginalized, and who themselves seek to live simply, élitist. A lay order whose concern is to transform society into one which reflects the kingdom community, and gives special attention to caring for the marginalized, cannot be termed an élitist body of people.

Likewise, the role and status of lay people who seek to blaze a trail in the communal transformation of society and, in the process, give time and energy to the encouragement of their colleagues to share in that calling, cannot be called élitist.

January 2018

8 Presbyters as a new order of continuity

Preamble

All the papers in this book argue for the urgency of a post-Christendom church bringing into being a renewed diaconate, the gift of God to the church to come. I have argued that the primary calling of a renewed diaconate is that of mission enablers, liberating the people of God for their vital kingdom community building ministry in today's fragmented world. I have also argued that the calling and work of a renewed diaconate would be of even more significance if, like the Methodist Diaconal Order, it took the form of a religious order.

Nevertheless, if the diaconal church is to be equipped with the kind of leadership it requires, the calling and role of presbyters also need radical re-appraisal. This paper discusses the societal, theological and ecclesiological context of such a re-appraisal, and sets out the meaning and implications of presbyters becoming 'an order of continuity', and possibly a religious order in their own right. As such, the calling and role of presbyters would become complementary to and of equal standing with that of a renewed diaconate. This means, in some churches, bringing an end to sequential ordination and to the anomaly of a transitional diaconate.

1 Introduction

1.1 The global context of the missional church

No church – national or local – exists for the preservation of its own life and work. Of course the church is called to 'make disciples'. However, its mission is not confined to 'the salvation of souls'. The church exists to enable society and world to become an integral part of the kingdom 'on earth as it is in heaven'. What that means in practice is not yet clear, in part because the church still remains captive to a Christendom understanding of the kingdom on earth. However, I believe that the creation of the world as some form of global community of communities is a divine imperative.

That the stakes are immensely high is indisputable. Humankind now has the power of either self-destruction or of building a world which survives and flourishes. In that context, the mission of the church is to offer humanity a vision of community at its zenith, and work with others to make that vision a reality.

1.2 The kingdom community

That vision of community at its zenith is what I call 'the kingdom community' (Clark, 2005). It is a community reflecting the nature of the Trinity and empowered by its communal gifts of life, liberation love and learning. It is a vision earthed in the message of the kingdom which Christ taught so much about, and which he lived out in his life, death and resurrection. It is also a vision which offers a new way of being human. It a kingdom which runs totally counter to what David Martin (2016) defines as 'the grain of the world'.

1.3 The diaconal church

If the church is to be an instrument of communal transformation, it has to become the servant of the kingdom community. This means it taking the form of a 'diaconal' or servant church. In turn, this requires that its leaders to become servant leaders, enabling church and world to be transformed by the gifts of the kingdom community. The church can have no authenticity and credibility in today's world unless the medium (of servant leadership) becomes the message.

1.4 The neighbourhood church

The mission of the diaconal church, through the laity as its primary mission resource, is to enable every human collective to manifest the gifts of the kingdom community. However, unless the gathered church exemplifies the presence of the gifts of the kingdom community (life, liberation, love and learning), the church as a whole cannot offer a vision of what human collectives transformed by those gifts might look like in practice. Nor can it equip its lay people with the insights, skills and resources to make secular kingdom communities a reality.

The neighbourhood church provides an essential 'home base' for the diaconal church. It looks to its past to enable the people of God to 're-member' their heritage in a way which can equip them for their ministry in the present and future. Here, church buildings can play an important role as 'symbolic places' which connect congregations, as well as the wider public, with the communal riches of the past. This is especially the case with Anglican churches which are often places resonant with history and examples of architectural beauty, as well as reminders of the long and resolute journey of those who have kept the faith over the centuries.

1.5 The leadership of the diaconal church – diaconal and presbyteral

I have argued in other papers that one essential form of leadership within the diaconal church will be a renewed diaconate as an order of mission. I have described the calling of deacons who will form this new order as that of 'mission enablers', a vocation that focuses on the transformation of human collectives throughout the whole of society.

However, to complement the creation of this new diaconal order of mission, the post-Christendom church will also need a renewed form of presbyteral leadership. Its responsibility will be to enable the neighbourhood church to manifest the gifts of the kingdom community. I interpret this as presbyters fulfilling their historic calling as 'an order of continuity' in a modern context.

2 Presbyters as an order of continuity

2.1 Continuity not maintenance

The primary calling of presbyters within the diaconal church is to ensure continuity, not engage in maintenance. Continuity seeks to employ the riches of the past in the service of present and future; maintenance seeks 'to keep the show on the road'. Continuity is about concern for both tradition and renewal; maintenance is about organizational survival. Continuity is concerned with strategic planning for the long-term and uses the liturgical, pastoral, and missiological resources of the past as a springboard to explore meaningful ways of being a diaconal church. Maintenance is too often about trying to preserve those forms and practices which reflect anachronistic memories, experiences and achievements. It is often captive to a Christendom model of church.

2.2 Neighbourhood or local presbyteral ministry

The normative focus of presbyteral ministry has been that of the parish or, in more sociological parlance, the neighbourhood. However, as a shortage of presbyters impacts on all denominations, many now exercise their ministry across a number of neighbourhoods and a number of gathered churches. What has been the norm for Methodist ministers is rapidly becoming the norm for other denominations. Nevertheless, I will continue to describe presbyters in this situation as 'neighbourhood' presbyters because their ministry remains focused on distinctive geographical areas, usually ones which can be identified as sociological entities where community of place often remains a strong bond.

The neighbourhood church today frequently draws members from a wide area. However, especially in the Church of England, with its awareness of parish boundaries, its main ministry is usually regarded as being to the neighbourhood in which the church is located.

A presbyteral ministry of continuity will be exercised through traditional routines, practices and events. However, within the diaconal church, this becomes a form of servant leadership whose overriding concern is to further the congregation's life and work as that which manifests the gifts of the kingdom community in traditional as well as innovative ways. Some responsibilities of a presbyter's calling as a ministry of continuity are set out below.

2.2.1 *Worship*

A presbyteral ministry of continuity draws on the spiritual riches of the past. However, it uses every opportunity to enrich the worshipping life of the neighbourhood church as a kingdom community in fresh and meaningful ways. In *The Kingdom at Work Project* (Clark, 2014), I suggest that worship, including the Eucharist, draws on the gifts of the kingdom community in a number of ways. These include:

- adoration, praise and thanksgiving – the gift of life;
- confession and forgiveness – the gift of liberation;
- intercession – the gift of love;
- 'the word' and reflection – the gift of learning;
- the offertory and dedication – a commitment to bear witness to all these gifts.

2.2.2 Education

Education should enable lay people to appreciate and explore the fundamentals of Christian faith. It should also be the gateway to enabling them to discern and use the gifts of the kingdom community – life, liberation, love and learning – to enrich daily life and work.

In the neighbourhood church, education comes to the fore notably through the proclaimed word, though the art of preaching is a much neglected skill. A preaching ministry of continuity draws on the insights of the past in order to shed light on what it means to discern and, in practice, further the gifts of the kingdom community in the present. Redemptive application of the 'word' to daily life is all too often ignored in sermons today.

Christian education benefits from being undertaken within small communal groups. However, the decline of such groups across all denominations has weakened the ability of the neighbourhood church to draw on the personal experience of church members in order to address current challenges to faith.

Overall, too much that is taken for 'education' within the neighbourhood church is little more than formal instruction. The latter fails to appreciate and build on the kingdom community's gift of learning as an exciting and rewarding journey of spiritual discovery (Clark, 2005, pp. 32-46).

2.2.3 Service

In the diaconal church, the presbyter encourages gathered church members to engage in service. This in particular witnesses to the kingdom's community's gift of love. As members of an order of continuity, presbyters can point to many examples of Christians who, in the past as well as present, have worked tirelessly to meet the needs of the poor, the marginalized and the disadvantaged.

2.2.4 Pastoral care

Here the neighbourhood church remains as an exemplar of the kingdom community's gift of love. Pastoral care can be greatly enriched where the presbyter shares pastoral responsibility for church and neighbourhood with lay members.

2.2.5 Symbolic place

As noted earlier, the church building, especially when of historic or architectural note, is often an important symbol of a common heritage and communal continuity for many people, including those who have diminishing links with the church. As an order of continuity, presbyters have a responsibility to ensure that the church building continues to fulfil this significant communal function as fully as possible (Clark, 1974).

2.2.6 Mission

Within the diaconal church, a renewed diaconate is complemented by a renewed presbyterate as facilitators of mission. However, the former are primarily concerned with equipping the laity, the dispersed church, for their ministry within the life of wider society. The presbyter's mission responsibilities focus on the continuity, renewal and growth of the neighbourhood church.

The responsibility of the presbyter for endeavours in mission may take a number of forms. One is 'planting' new churches, often employing established neighbourhood churches as springboards for such initiatives. Another is furthering 'fresh expressions of church'. These may arise within an existing neighbourhood church (for example, in the form of 'messy church'), or occur beyond the neighbourhood church (for example, as some kind of new Christian group). However, within the diaconal church, the hall mark of the presbyter's mission endeavours is that they manifest the gifts of the kingdom community.

2.2.7 Representation

The deacon, as a member of an order of mission, represents the diaconal church primarily as a movement. The presbyter, as a member of an order of continuity, represents the diaconal church primarily as an institution. In this context, the presbyter may well become a symbolic person helping to enhance a sense of community within the neighbourhood.

3 The relationship of presbyters as an order of continuity to deacons as an order of mission

3.1 Continuity and mission

Servant leadership within the diaconal church is concerned with both continuity and mission. These two tasks embody the responsibilities of presbyters and deacons. They hold together the diaconal church's continuity as an institution and its mission as a movement for transformation. Both deacon and presbyter exercise their leadership in the service of the kingdom community and its gifts of life, liberation, love and learning.

However, the problem here is that the church, captive to so many anachronistic aspects of Christendom, continues to seek continuity and engage in mission in ways related to an ecclesiology which is well past its sell-by date. This means that, whilst always affirming the riches of the past, Christians need to be open to new ways of being church, with the diaconal model of church being a model of paramount importance.

3.2 Beyond a hierarchy of ministries

The diaconal model of church is founded on the belief that the church is the servant of the kingdom community. That model means that the church and its leaders are likewise servants of the kingdom. Whether their leadership function is continuity or mission, diaconal church leaders are also servants of the people of God, those called to be at the forefront of the mission of the church in the world.

Within the diaconal church, servant leadership may continue to take the shape of a three-fold form of ordained ministry: deacon, presbyter and bishop. This honours church tradition, whilst offering a new and important division of labour for the church to come. However, a diaconal ecclesiology rules out any form of hierarchy which clones the Christendom model of church. It challenges the authenticity of so-called 'sequential ordination' in which ordination is regarded as a person moving from 'a lower' (diaconal) to 'a higher' (presbyteral or episcopal) order. Consequently a diaconal ecclesiology cannot embrace any form of 'transitional diaconate' where diaconal ministry is treated as a brief period of 'probation' for presbyteral ministry.

117

In the diaconal church all forms of ordained ministry are 'full and equal orders' (Barnett, 1995). All are servants of the kingdom community and of the people of God. Deacon, presbyter and bishop, though having different roles and responsibilities, are called to be servant leaders with similar ecclesiological standing. Their ministry is fundamentally collaborative and co-operative. All are representatives of the church within the wider world.

Where a hierarchical ecclesiology remains in place, the life and mission of the church are compromised because such an ecclesiology fails to reflect the nature of the kingdom community. It is a form of ecclesiology which ignores the increasing adoption of the model of servant leadership within society (Greenleaf, 1970). A hierarchical ecclesiology has always tempted the church to usurp the primacy of the kingdom, and to regard the maintenance of the former as being more important than the coming of the latter. If this happens, whether the church grows numerically or not, it will be a hindrance to the eventual coming of the kingdom and the communal transformation of society.

4 A presbyteral order of continuity as a religious order

In Paper 5, I set out the case for a diaconal order of mission taking the form of a religious order. This is important for a number of reasons. First, in a ministry which is about the transformation of society, deacons are often out on their own initiating intervention in very difficult circumstances. The secular world is frequently hostile to the values of the kingdom community and seeks to ignore or negate them whenever they challenge its pre-occupation with power and wealth. Thus the communal support of fellow deacons is an immense asset. Secondly, a religious community which embraces the gifts of the kingdom community can offer a model, however limited by human fallibilities, of the meaning of community at its zenith.

For similar reasons, presbyters should be offered the opportunity of becoming members of a religious order of their own. The role of the presbyter is not easy to fulfil in this day and age and such a supportive community could be of great benefit to him or her. Furthermore, as just noted, being part of a religious order seeking to manifest the gifts of the kingdom community offers a model to church and world, alongside that of a renewed diaconate as a religious order, of what it means to be a kingdom community.

However, two provisos need to be added. One is that membership of a presbyteral religious order needs to be optional. The other is that, with a potentially large membership, a presbyteral religious order would need to be sub-divided into regions, co-ordinated and overseen by a number of full-time 'officers' chosen by the members of that order.

---

5 Methodism and Methodist presbyters as an order of continuity

5.1 Methodism as a diaconal church

British Methodism today embraces many significant hall-marks of the diaconal church. For example:

- o Methodism retains many features of its origins as a holiness movement, a concept which embraces the gifts of the kingdom community [see Appendix].
- o Within Methodism, lay people are regarded as the church's primary mission resource. As stated in its *Deed of Union*, the ministries of lay and ordained are held to be of equal standing.
- o Methodism is a profoundly communal church with a strong emphasis on 'fellowship' and pastoral care.
- o Methodism is a mutually supportive 'Connexion' (*The Gift of Connexionalism*, 2017).
- o Authority within Methodism lies with its Conference as a corporate body of lay and ordained representatives.
- o Methodism has always had a deep concern for the poor and marginalized as an essential focus of mission.
- o The Methodist Church in Britain has consistently been in the van of the ecumenical movement.

These hall-marks make it easier for Methodism than for some other churches to move towards a diaconal form of church and of servant leadership. However, Methodism has not always appreciated the importance of the deeply communal nature of its theology and the diaconal character of its ecclesiology. Thus it remains in danger of neglecting or losing that which could offer a great deal to the church to come. This is all the more reason why Methodism should become more aware of its precious diaconal resources and thus be able to blaze a diaconal trail for every denomination. [I expand on this issue in Paper 9.]

5.2 The Methodist Diaconal Order as a new order of mission

In Papers 3 and 4, I set out the reasons why I believe that the diaconate should today assume the calling of a new order of mission. I also indicate there why the Methodist Diaconal Order, as an order of ministry *and* a religious order, is in pole positon to develop further in this direction, and what would be the implications of such a change for Methodism and the wider church.

5.3 Methodist presbyters as an order of continuity

However, to complement the emergence of the Methodist Diaconal Order as an order of mission, Methodist presbyters need to become an order of continuity with a primarily neighbourhood-focused form of ministry.

5.3.1 The legacy of Methodism

Methodism began as a movement *alongside* an established ecclesiastical institution. Methodist ministers, unlike parish priests, were never intended to have 'pastoral charge' of a single church and its surrounding area. They were itinerant animators and encouragers, riding long distances on horseback, serving small congregations (societies) networked within loosely defined boundaries (circuits). During their travels, such ministers would often stop and preach to gatherings of those with few if any links to the established church.

However, over the years, all branches of Methodism became increasingly institutionalized. Their form and flexibility as movements disappeared. Consequently, the roles and responsibilities of Methodist ministers also grew more formal and grounded. Their responsibilities gradually became less missional and more focused on the worship, pastoral care and administrative needs of the local churches (societies) assigned to their care. Thus most Methodist ministers became 'neighbourhood presbyters'. Their calling in many ways came to clone that of the parish priest, though with responsibility for more churches, often small in membership, and spread over an area a good deal larger than a parish.

5.3.2 Methodist presbyters as an order of continuity within a diaconal church

Nevertheless, Methodism and Methodist leadership continue to embody many of the hall-marks of the diaconal church. For example, Methodist presbyters are received into 'Full Connexion', a practice affirming the interconnected and communal nature of the Methodist Church, ordained and lay alike. Thus Methodist presbyters are well placed to demonstrate what it would mean to become an order of continuity within a diaconal church, an order concerned to enable the neighbourhood church to manifest ever more fully the gifts of life, liberation, love and learning.

5.3.3 Mission

The missional calling of Methodist presbyters as an order of continuity would remain that of building up the neighbourhood church, of facilitating the planting of churches wherever appropriate and of fostering fresh expressions of church within or beyond the institutional church. As leaders of a diaconal church, all these endeavours would be measured against the extent to which they gave expression to the gifts of the kingdom community.

5.3.4 Transferring from presbyteral to diaconal ministry

As and when the diaconal church becomes a reality, it is likely that some Methodist presbyters will choose to transfer to the Methodist Diaconal Order. One reason for this is that the diaconate, as a new order of mission, replicates and reflects not only the early heritage of Methodism as a mission movement, but the latter's impressive commitment, in the late nineteenth century, to promoting a social gospel. The normative nature of such transfers would be enhanced if, as I have argued in other papers in this book, a renewed order of deacons were to be given authority to celebrate holy communion, even if this occurred only occasionally.

5.3.5 A Methodist presbyteral religious order

It would be important for Methodist presbyters to have the opportunity of becoming members of a Methodist presbyteral religious order, for reasons given in section 4 above. The historical significance of this is underlined by the fact that 'one of the original emphases of the body

121

of Mr. Wesley's preachers and helpers which eventually developed into the body of Methodist Ministers (presbyters)... (was) something like a religious order' (*What is a Presbyter?*, 2002, section 11).

6 The ecumenical imperative

The church to come will be diaconal. It will also be ecumenical, because a church which is the servant of the kingdom community cannot be divided or divisive. In the British context, this means that, amongst other manifestations of ecumenicity, it is imperative and urgent that Methodism and the Church of England continue to strive to 'get their act together'. [See Paper 9 for my review of the most recent attempt to create an interchangeability of presbyteral ministries.]

In the diaconal church to come, Anglican and Methodist presbyters would come together as an ecumenical order of continuity focused on enabling the neighbourhood church to manifest the gifts of the kingdom community. At the same time, it would be important for Methodist presbyters in particular to remain open to moving into a renewed diaconal order of mission. As noted above, this would be an affirmation of their ecclesiological heritage.

August 2017

9 A diaconal response to 'Mission and Ministry in Covenant' A report from the Faith and Order bodies of the Church of England and the Methodist Church[1]

Preamble

'Conversations' about the unity of the Church of England and the British Methodist Church have been going on for most of my lifetime. In the 1960s, whilst a Methodist presbyter in circuit, I argued passionately for acceptance of the Anglican-Methodist Unity Scheme then under consideration by both churches. I was greatly disappointed by the rejection of that scheme by the House of Clergy in 1969, and by a similar outcome in 1972.

In 1982, a Covenanting for Unity proposal, which included the Methodist, Moravian the Reformed churches in Britain, again failed to receive the support of the Anglican General Synod.

In 1994, the Methodist Church approached the Church of England to begin 'unity' talks afresh. These got underway two years later. In 2001, an 'Anglican-Methodist Covenant' for unity was agreed by both churches. It was signed, in 2003, in the presence of the Queen in the Methodist Central Hall, Westminster. Since then a Joint Implementation Commission (JIC) has produced a plethora of reports, culminating, in 2014, in 'The Challenge of the Covenant'. This contained a number of recommendations accepted by both churches. Two key ones were that:

- o the Methodist Church… consider afresh expressing the Conference's ministry of oversight in a personal form of connexional, episcopal ministry and the Church of England… recognise… ministry in the Methodist Church as a sign of continuity in faith, worship and mission in a church that is in the apostolic succession;
- o the Church of England and the Methodist Church… address the question of reconciling, with integrity, the existing

---

[1] www.churchofengland.org/sites/default/.../mission-and-ministry-in-covenant.pdf

presbyteral and diaconal ministries of our two churches, which would lead to the interchangeability of ministries.

Mission and Ministry in Covenant (2018) is the report of the Faith and Order bodies of both churches, which took over the responsibilities of the JIC, offering a way in which the latter's recommendations could be implemented. In 2018, this report, with a number of recommendations agreed in the light of the initial discussions in both assemblies, was accepted for ongoing consideration by the General Synod of the Church of England and the Methodist Conference.

1 Introduction –
A summary of the report

1.1 The report – chapter one

The first chapter of *Mission and Ministry in Covenant* sets the context for the proposals of the chapters that follow by showing how they are grounded… 'in the 2003 Covenant commitments' already made (3)[1]. The chapter notes the affirmations of, and subsequent commitments associated with the Covenant of 2003. It then offers a number of steps which go further than the latter and would commit both churches (1):

- o 'to share the ministry of the historic episcopate as a sign of the apostolicity of the Church of God;
- o to welcome all presbyters/priests serving in either church as eligible to serve in both churches.'

The reports states that:

In particular, the Methodist Church will need to find a way to receive the ministry of the historic episcopate, while the Church of England will need to find a way to enable Methodist presbyters not ordained by a bishop within the historic episcopate to exercise ordained ministry within the Church of England by invitation. (14)

The report notes that consideration of the interchangeability of diaconal ministries 'must await continuing dialogue among all the churches concerning the nature of diaconal ministry and is therefore beyond the scope of this present report'. (15)

---

[1] Numbers in brackets refer to the sections of *Mission and Ministry in Covenant*.

In a reference to the contemporary context of mission, the report states that:

> Sharing the gospel in a country whose ethnic and cultural diversity continues to grow presents particular challenges. Likewise, the global situation of poverty and violence makes it urgent for Christians to speak and act together. All this indicates that deepening relationships of communion on the way to the full visible unity of the Church are essential for the effective proclamation of the gospel that the world might believe. (18)

1.2 The report – chapter two

The second chapter of the report considers how Methodism 'might share the ministry of the historic episcopate as a sign of the apostolicity of the Church of God' and 'what it would mean for the Methodist Church to express the Conference's ministry of oversight in a personal form of Connexional, episcopal ministry in such a way that the Methodist Church can be recognized by Anglican churches as sharing in the historic episcopate'. (1)

The report 'affirms that the idea developed by the JIC of a "President-bishop" can be accepted by Anglicans as an instance of the historic episcopate "locally adapted in the methods of its administration to the varying needs of the nations and peoples called of God into the unity of His Church".' (4) The report argues that this idea 'fits with the distinctive theology and self-understanding of the Methodist Church, and in particular the centrality of the Conference for *episkope*.' (4)

The process of electing a Methodist President-bishop would be as follows. (44)

- o In year one, the Methodist President for the coming year would be ordained to the episcopate by at least three Anglican bishops. The Methodist President-bishop would preside at the ordination of all new presbyters and deacons (as would President-bishops in succeeding years).
- o In year two, the next Methodist President-bishop would be ordained to the episcopate by the ex-President-bishop of year one and two or more Anglican bishops.
- o In year three, the next Methodist President-bishop would be

ordained to the episcopate by the two existing ex-President-bishops and one or more Anglian bishops.

o In following years the ex-President Methodist bishops would preside at the ordination of future President-bishops.

1.3 The report – chapter three

'The third chapter focuses on the second commitment, to welcome all presbyters/priests serving in either church as eligible to serve in both churches… It considers the particular question of how the Church of England could offer such a welcome to all Methodist presbyters, given its historic commitment to the norm of episcopal ordination for all priests'. (5)

In addressing this question, the proposals draw on the concept of 'anomaly', as understood in Anglican ecumenical thinking. In brief, this concept means that the Church of England would accept all existing Methodist presbyters as authorized to minister in both churches, even though the latter had not been episcopally ordained. This would be a 'temporary' expedient as, after a number of years, there would be no Methodist presbyters who had not been ordained into the historic episcopate.

The report acknowledges that consequently:

There may… be a need for churches moving deeper into unity with one another to be ready to endure certain temporary anomalies in their arrangements as part of the journey towards unity, without abandoning the norms with regard to which anomalies can be identified. In this case, accepting that the journey involves bearing a particular anomaly on the part of the Church of England affirms that there is no intention to undermine or dilute the Church of England's commitment to the Anglican norm, shared with the Roman Catholic and Orthodox churches, of episcopal ordination. (58)

However, 'this aspect of the report's proposals rests on the recognition already given by the Church of England to the Methodist Church's (existing) ordained ministries and to its (existing) exercise of oversight…' (5)

1.4 The report – chapter four

This chapter gives a brief overview of legislative changes needed to put the report's proposals into effect in both churches. It also sets out a provisional timetable for how the proposals it contains might be taken through the requisite processes of approval in both churches. (6)

The ecumenical imperative
A personal note

Nothing in Paper 9 is meant to indicate that I have anything but the deepest of commitments to the ecumenical imperative. My life's work, not least my passion for the creation of a renewed diaconate, has been focused on the emergence of a diaconal church which would possess a profound sense of Christian unity and solidarity in commitment, spirit and practice. I believe that the emergence of the church to come, the diaconal church, is both an ecumenical and divine imperative not only for the whole Christian community, but for a world and planet increasingly in danger of self-destruction.

This is not to argue that even a diaconal church has to be homogeneous in all facets of its theology and ecclesiology. However, in every way that matters in terms of mission and ministry, such a church must be communally whole. Thus I concur with the Anglican-Methodist International Commission (*Into all the world*, AMICUM, section 127) that, hitherto, 'our separation has diminished each of us'.

Nonetheless, such an ecumenical imperative does not mean that we engage on a quest for unity at all costs. In this paper, I argue that, unless the report's recommendations for the interchangeability of ministries take us nearer the emergence of the diaconal church, they will ultimately be more of a hindrance than a help. Therefore, many of the criticisms of the report raised below are related to whether or not its recommendations enhance or weaken the hall-marks of the church to come, not least that of God's gift of a renewed diaconate.

---

2 The limitations of *Mission and Ministry in Covenant* – a diaconal perspective

2.1 A failure to address the critical context of mission

One weakness of this report is that there is only a single brief paragraph (18) addressing the importance of Christian unity in the context of Christians needing to be better equipped to face the needs of today's world. This is quite inadequate given that humankind is, for the first time in its history, facing the real possibility of self-destruction.

I acknowledge that a report of this kind does not have the space to set out the context of mission today at any great length. However, an inadequate missional framework fails to bring home to the reader the dire consequences of certain challenges which humankind now faces, not least the misuse of nuclear power and the failure to check global warming. Exacerbating such challenges is the ongoing failure to create a world which is a global community of communities. This neglect of a misssional context weakens the motivation needed to inspire and empower the Christian community to come together to address far-reaching societal and global concerns in a credible and effective way.

2.2 The neglect or misinterpretation of the Methodist *Deed of Union*

The Methodist *Deed of Union* of 1932 (Section 2, Clause 4) states explicitly that:

> Presbyters… hold no priesthood differing in kind from that which is common to all the Lord's people and they have no exclusive title to the preaching of the gospel or the care of souls. These ministries are shared with them by others to whom also the Spirit divides his gifts severally as he wills…

> The Methodist Church holds the doctrine of the priesthood of all believers and consequently believes that no priesthood exists which belongs exclusively to a particular order or class of persons… For the sake of church order and not because of any priestly virtue inherent in the office the presbyters of the Methodist Church are set apart by ordination to the ministry of the word and sacraments.

Based on these affirmations, it needs to be re-stated quite clearly that, for the Methodist Church, the ministries of presbyters, deacons and lay people are (theologically) of equal standing. This is a principle which lies at the very heart of Methodism's ecclesiology as a Connexional system. It is also a principle which underpins all the ministries, ordained and lay, of the diaconal church.

For some years the Faith and Order Committee of Methodism has contended that acceptance of the historic episcopate would not violate the fundamental principles of the *Deed of Union*. In my view, many of their arguments[1] come over as casuistic. For example, in their 1982 report to Conference[1], the Committee states that: '... acceptance of the historic episcopate is not to be equated with belief in the apostolic succession'. (16) I wonder how many Anglicans would accept that statement.

The Committee also adds that '... we (Methodists) are not asked to believe that bishops are essential to validate the Church, but we are asked to accept the historic episcopate as necessary for the promotion of unity' (16). This seems to me to be arguing that the end (interchangeability of ministries) justifies the means (taking episcopacy into the Methodist system). Vital as achieving reciprocal ordained ministries may be, I believe that such a way forward would undermine the historic ecclesiology of both Methodism and, vital for the long-term future, the diaconal church.

It is perhaps noteworthy that *Mission and Ministry in Covenant* does not mention these key clauses of the *Deed of Union* (though they have been addressed in previous reports of the Faith and Order Committee to Conference). It would seem that, for some reason, the report writers do not wish to bring to the fore again what I believe are fundamental theological principles which have undergirded Methodism's understandings of the nature of ministry for many years.

2.3 The existing status of Methodist presbyters and deacons as being an 'anomaly'

The suggestion that the ordination of existing Methodist presbyters and deacons has somehow been an 'anomaly' (a term which appears seventeen times in the report) is extraordinary if we accept the common

---

[1] For example, *Episcopacy and Methodist Doctrinal Standards* (1982) Report of the Faith and Order Committee to the Methodist Conference

meaning of 'anomaly' as an 'irregularity of motion or behaviour'[1].

On the one hand, the report argues that regarding past Methodist ordinations as such an anomaly is something that should be accepted as 'bearable when there is an agreed goal of visible unity' (56) at stake. The assumption here seems to be that it is the Church of England that is making the sacrifice. My own conviction is that most of the 'bearing' is being asked of existing Methodist presbyters and deacons, both active and supernumerary.

On the other hand, the report admits that 'it would be inappropriate to use the term "anomaly" regarding anyone's ordination' (57). The strange justification for doing just that, is that the situation would be 'temporary'. However, on any reckoning, it would take at least 40 years before all living Methodist presbyters were episcopally ordained, whilst, in the process, creating a two-tier 'status' amongst Methodist presbyters. Far from the period of the anomaly being 'a moment of grace' (73), as the report hopes, for not a few Methodist presbyters and deacons it could feel more like a prolonged period of 'dis-grace'.

2.4 The marginalization of the permanent diaconate

Because the report, if accepted, is in grave danger of introducing a hierarchical form of ordained ministry into Methodism, one of its potentially destructive outcomes would be the marginalization of the permanent diaconate in both churches. That situation would, in turn, lead to both churches continuing to turn their back on a renewed diaconate as offering an urgently needed new form of leadership, that of mission enabler, for the church present and future. It would also deny the emergence of a renewed diaconate as what I believe is a gift of God to the church to come, a gift slowly being recognized and employed in mission by many churches worldwide.

A late notice of motion accepted at the Methodist Conference of 2018 could mean that the place of the permanent diaconate will (at least from the Methodist side) be considered in current discussions about the interchangeability of ministries. Such a motion was needed because the report argued that 'any proposals regarding diaconal ministries must await continuing dialogue amongst all churches concerning the nature

---

[1] *Concise Oxford Dictionary*

of diaconal ministry' (15). 'Interchangeability of deacons' (sic) would depend on 'a common understanding of diaconal ministry' (95 (b)), but only when both churches could get round to considering what was apparently deemed to be a relatively minor matter.

2.4.1 *The diaconate as 'a full and equal order'*

The position taken in all the papers in this book is the very opposite of that taken by the report. It is that the neither of our churches will be able to realize the potential of future presbyteral ministry until they grasp the importance of the diaconate as 'a full and equal order'[1]. There are a number of issues to be addressed here. The first, as argued in Paper 2, is that the (amended) *Deed of Union* (Section 2, Clause 4) is behind the times when it states that:

> Christ's ministers in the church are stewards in the household of God and shepherds of his flock. Some are called and ordained to this occupation as presbyters or deacons. *Presbyters have a principal and directing part in these great duties...* [my italics].

Neither in 1932, when the *Deed of Union* was adopted, nor in 1976 when the word 'deacon' was added to this clause, had Methodism recognised deacons as an order of ministry. This change of status for the diaconate was only agreed by the Methodist Conference in 1993, and confirmed when all deacons were received into Full Connexion in 1998. My conviction, therefore, is that since 1993, Methodist presbyters should no longer be regarded as having 'a principal and directing' role as church leaders, an anachronistic view repeated by this report (51). In the diaconal church to come, any continuing three-fold form of ministry will exercise servant leadership as full and equal partners, though with different roles and responsibilities reflecting the changing needs of church and society. Thus it is essential that any consideration of the interchangeability of ministries must, from now on, include the diaconate.

2.4.2 *The need to end a transitional diaconate*

If a renewed diaconate is to be 'a full and equal order' alongside other forms of ordained ministry, the transitional diaconate becomes an

---

[1] A notable phrase used by Barnett in *The Diaconate: a Full and Equal Order* (first published 1981)

anachronism. It is not existing Methodist ministries which should be regarded as an 'anomaly', as the report suggests, but the idea and practice of a transitional diaconate.

William Ditewig, a leading Roman Catholic deacon in the United States, writes that from the fifth century onwards the diaconate, hitherto a leadership calling of considerable importance in the early church, steadily declined (p. 75). A key reason for this was 'the development of the idea of the *cursus honorum*' within the church of the Constantinian era. The *cursus honorum* was imported from the Roman civil administration and indicated a succession of grades through which one progressed from the lower to the higher. Thus the practice of 'rising through the ranks', in the form of sequential ordination, began increasingly to shape the ordained leadership of Christendom from that era onwards.

With the decline of the office of deacon and the elevation of the office of priest (presbyter), for many centuries the former became a formal and normatively short step en route to the latter. However, as the reinstatement of a permanent diaconate has of late come about in many churches, it is being gradually recognized that neither a renewed diaconate nor a renewed presbyterate can emerge unless the anomaly of the transitional deacon is addressed.

William Ditewig, from a Roman Catholic perspective, argues (p. 209) that 'it is reasonable to postulate that it will be only with the overcoming of the remaining vestiges of the medieval *cursus honorum* that the normative, permanent diaconate will continue its proper development'. Michael Jackson (2018, pp. 39-41), a long-standing and influential deacon in the Anglican Church of Canada, likewise contends that 'the church should return to its original practice, end sequential ordination and abolish the transitional diaconate which serves little purpose and inhibits the ministry of the vocational deacon'. More recently, James Newcome, Bishop of Carlisle (2018), has expressed the view that 'calling probationary priests deacons simply compromises the integrity of the diaconate and degrades the office... It therefore seems very hard to justify retaining a "transitional diaconate".'

This is an issue which needs to be urgently addressed by all churches, but first and foremost by the Church of England, where the transitional diaconate is still the norm, if the potential of presbyteral and diaconal ministries is to be realized and greater interchangeability of ministries be beneficial.

2.4.3 *A renewed diaconate as mission enablers*

I believe that another reason why the report now needs to bring a renewed diaconate into the frame is that this form of church leadership is a divine imperative for the creation of a new and invaluable resource for mission. As I have contended in many of the papers in this book, the calling of God's gift of a renewed diaconate is that of the enabler of the people of God in their ministry and mission in the world. This means moving away from the past understanding of the diaconate as corralled by a ministry of service, to its taking the lead in equipping and educating the laity for mission in daily life. Thus a renewed diaconate becomes the lead order for the church dispersed in the world, complementary to the presbyterate as the lead order for the church gathered.

Anglican and Methodist Churches elsewhere have grasped the potential of a renewed diaconate far more fully than those in the UK. For example, in 2017, the Anglican Church of Canada had some 400 deacons and the Episcopal Church in the USA some 3000 deacons (Jackson, p. 15). In contrast, the Church of England has some 100 active permanent deacons. This is 'hardly a ringing endorsement of the diaconate', as Michael Jackson comments (p. 15). In 2018, the British Methodist Church had 136 active and student deacons, and 118 retired deacons.[1] In contrast, the United Methodist Church in the USA has over 2500 active deacons, and 600 retired deacons.

2.4.5 *The Methodist Diaconal Order as a religious order*

In any future consideration of the interchangeability of diaconal ministries, the Faith and Order bodies of both churches should take into consideration the potential gift to an Anglican diaconate of its deacons becoming members of a religious order, reflecting the life and work of the Methodist Diaconal Order as a religious order.

2.5 Stretching the meaning of episkope

The importance of Section 2, Clause 4 of the Methodist *Deed of Union* comes especially to the fore in two other hall-marks of Methodist

---

[1] Report to the Methodist Conference, 2018

ecclesiology. Because 'the Methodist Church holds the doctrine of the priesthood of all believers and consequently believes that no priesthood exists which belongs exclusively to a particular order or class of persons', Methodism's ecclesiology is essentially communal. Hence the British Methodist Church has the unique character of being a 'Connexion', a gift to the church to come recognized in the report (32).

I have argued elsewhere that not only is Methodism's ecclesiology fundamentally communal, but so too is its theology of mission. For example, I believe that Methodism's espousal of 'social holiness', a key aspect of its theology of mission, can be equated today with what I have termed a theology of 'communal holiness' [see Appendix].

However, since the acceptance of *Baptism, Eucharist and Ministry* (the Lima Document) by the World Council of Churches in 1982, three forms of authority and oversight have come to the fore – the 'personal', 'the collegial' and 'the communal' (or 'corporate'). The Faith and Order Committee of Methodism has tried to argue that Methodist ecclesiology (including the Methodist Conference) embraces communal *and* personal oversight.[1] This is also argued in sections 34-36 of *Mission and Ministry in Covenant*. Section 36 focuses on what is deemed to be the personal authority of the President of Conference, implying that Methodism thus embraces both communal *and* personal forms of *episkope*. The conclusion is that Methodist ecclesiology is thus able to accept the idea of the historic episcopate, where personal oversight is dominant.

I believe this is stretching the meaning of *episkope* to breaking point. It is clear that, in Methodism, authority and oversight are fundamentally *communal*, and thus accord with the ecclesiology of the diaconal church. In the Church of England, they are essentially personal, and to some extent collegial (as in the case of the House of Bishops), but certainly not communal. These very important differences should be openly recognized and grappled with in order to discover their potential value, or otherwise, to the ecclesiology of the church of the future.

---

[1] *Episcopacy (1998)*, Faith and Order Report to the Methodist Conference (44d)

2.6 The primacy of the people of God as a mission resource is not recognized

Section 2, Clause 4 of the Methodist *Deed of Union* has one further implication which receives scant attention in *Mission and Ministry in Covenant*, dominated as it is by the issue of the interchangeability of the ministries of presbyters. The *Deed of Union* underlines that Methodism has always stressed the primacy of the laity in the life and mission of the church, and equal partners with those ordained. However, Methodism, especially Wesleyan Methodism, has not infrequently drifted towards clericalism. It is a danger evident in Methodism's recent attraction to chaplaincy, mainly involving those ordained, as a key form of mission in a secular society. Such clericalism runs counter to what has always been at the heart of Methodist ecclesiology; the primacy of the laity as the church's primary mission resource[1]. Fascination with ordained chaplaincy can all too easily result in a failure to recognize and equip lay people for their ministry in daily life.

The primacy of the people of God in Methodist ecclesiology is reflected in a letter sent to me by a former Chairman of District who served on the commission considering *The Ministry of the People of God in the World*. He quotes[2] from the commission's files:

> We want to assert that the ministry of the whole people of God in the world is both the primary and normative ministry of the church. By primary we mean it comes first. By normative we mean that it is the basic model of discipleship. Therefore, instead of trying to define ministry in terms of ordination, we should be starting from the opposite end. That is we should define the priesthood of the ordained in terms of the priesthood of all the faithful, within which the priesthood of the ordained is a specialisation.

The primacy of the laity as a mission resource is fundamental to the ecclesiology of Methodism. Unless this is accepted, the closer association of ordained ministries will be of little worth.

---

[1] Note here two still influential reports to the Methodist Conference: *The Ministry of the People of God* (1988) and *The Ministry of the People of God in the World* (1990)

[2] In personal correspondence from the Revd Donald Eadie (6/3/18), a former Chairman of the Birmingham Methodist District.

2.7 Other aspects of the report

There are a number of other aspects of *Mission and Ministry in Covenant* which find it wanting.

2.7.1 There is little analysis of the meaning of mission in a secular context

Although the word 'mission' appears many times in the report, there is little consideration of what this means for either the Methodist or Anglican Church and where there is or is not common ground. This, in turn, means that no clear or inspiring vision is offered of the nature of the church to come and of its mission task which makes the closer bonding of church leadership so imperative.

2.7.2 There is no vision of the benefits of the interchangeability of ministries

Apart from the assumption that the interchangeability of ministries is a good thing, few of its specific benefits are spelled out in the report. For example, how would such a development enhance mission endeavours, not least through any re-deployment of presbyters across both churches and the shared use of physical plant?

2.7.3 How interchangeability of ministries would affect each church's future relations with their sister churches is not considered.

Although there is a short section about ecumenical schemes which have been undertaken elsewhere, notably in North and South India [71-73], little is said about how the proposals of *Mission and Ministry in Covenant* might affect, positively or negatively, the relations of both churches with their existing partners (98).

2.7.4 There is no mention of the Established status of the Church of England and what position Methodist presbyters (episcopally ordained or otherwise) would have in a church with such a status.

It is uncertain what status Methodist 'President-bishops' would have in this context, as well as what would be their public standing in relation to bishops in the Church of England.

2.7.5 The process for episcopally ordaining Methodist presbyters and deacons appears contrived, long-term and potentially divisive.

The means for the transition to interchangeability of presbyters is summarised above [1.2 of this paper]. The process (44) set out comes over as a somewhat contrived form of 'double-act' between Presidents of Conference and Anglican bishops. The artificiality of this process makes it hard to believe that it will be taken seriously by the Methodist Conference, not least its lay members, and by the Methodist people as a whole. Furthermore, the process makes it appear as if, far from offering Methodism a precious gift (the historic episcopate), the Church of England is legitimizing the ministry of future presbyters and deacons in a way that could become exclusive and potentially divisive for existing presbyters and deacons not in a position to receive this new status.

2.7.6 An apparent acknowledgement during the presentation of the report to the Methodist Conference of 2018, that Methodist presbyters and Anglican priests unhappy with the Covenant may be permitted to opt out of the interchangeability of ministries, would threaten any positive attributes of the whole process.

It is not clear whether this was a 'throw away' comment at the Methodist Conference representing a situation agreed by both churches. However, if accurate, such an option would potentially lead to serious divisions

3 An alternative way forward

3.1 The benchmark of any ecumenical endeavour should be whether or not it furthers the emergence of the diaconal church

There is little doubt that the pressure to produce proposals for the interchangeability of Methodist and Anglican presbyteral ministries has increased in recent years, not least because both churches are facing a severe decline in membership and in the number of those offering for ordination. The well documented 2018 edition of *UK Church Statistics* projects that, by 2022, membership of the Church of England will have fallen to just over one million (a decline of 14% from 2017) and that of Methodism to just over 160,000 (a decline of 18% from 2017). Such decline has been going on for many decades. The loss of members and fall in the number of presbyters is particularly acute within Methodism.

However, even accepting that the interchangeability of ministries on the basis of the proposals in this report might, in the short term, give a greater sense of togetherness, there are few indications that it will stem this ongoing decline. For one thing, these proposals are too little too late: in the 1960s the achievement of organic unity might conceivably have led to a very different future for both churches. For another, these proposals do not address the real challenge facing the church in a post-modern era: that is, how to discover and espouse a theology of mission and an ecclesiology which can make a new and credible contribution to the salvation of a world in crisis. It is my contention in these papers that such a theology has to be a kingdom theology and such an ecclesiology a diaconal ecclesiology, both embodied within and expressed through a diaconal church. Thus what really matters is not the numerical decline of inherited churches, but what they can offer and how they can co-operate to enable a diaconal church to come into being.

3.2 Identifying and affirming hall-marks of a diaconal church already present in both churches

A number of hall-marks of the diaconal church already present within Methodism have been spelt out in this and previous papers. They include a theology of mission founded on the pursuit of communal holiness [see Appendix], an ecclesiology of a fundamentally communal nature, the primacy of the people of God as a resource for mission, and a laity and ordained ministry which work together to manifest what it means to be the priesthood of all believers.

All the papers in this book have stressed that one other extremely important potential contribution of Methodism to the diaconal church is the Methodist Diaconal Order, as both an order of mission and a religious order. This too is facing challenges and changes, but it has within it the potential to play a key role in the leadership of the diaconal church, the church of the future.

The contribution of the Church of England to the diaconal church is less easy to identify, not least because the former remains very much moulded by a Christendom model of church. I do not believe that the historic episcopate is such a contribution, valuable as it may have been in the past. Nor does the Methodist Church believe this. The Conference of 1997 agreed 'that episcopacy is not essential to the church'[1].

On the other hand, the Church of England has important assets which would enhance the life and mission of a diaconal church. First

---

[1] *Episcopacy (1998)* Faith and Order Report to the Methodist Conference, (44a)

is its parish system which is founded on the principle that no person, whatever their creed, class or circumstances, is beyond the grace of God and membership of the kingdom. Secondly, the Anglican liturgy, in its spiritual depth and embracing of symbolic Christian events and festivals, offers a key contribution to the worship of the church to come. Thirdly, many Anglican churches, not least its cathedrals, and the music and art which they have inspired down the ages, are symbolic places of immense importance for a diaconal church which must not lose touch with its rich Christian heritage.

3.3 Another way forward

Where, then, do we go from here? I am convinced that the way forward is not to force together the ministries of the British Methodist Church and Church of England in a way which would not only compromise deeply held beliefs and principles, but hamper the emergence of the diaconal church to come. That can only lead to further fractures and hostilities. It would also alienate those sister churches with which both denominations are at the moment in creative partnership.

An alternative way forward is to continue to go with the ecumenical flow where it is strongest. This means that we affirm and pursue those ecumenical initiatives which have so far proved of real value, notably where there has been a genuine commitment by the leadership of not only the Anglican and Methodist Churches, but other denominations as well, 'to get their act together'.

As one example, I would point to the model of Churches Together in Cumbria, the first so-called 'ecumenical county in England'. In 2011, church leaders from the Methodist, United Reformed and Anglican Churches signed an historic 'Declaration of Intent' to worship, work and mission together in every way possible. In 2016, these Churches were joined by the Salvation Army in signing a 'Declaration of Covenant Partnership', whilst those from the Roman Catholic and Baptist Churches, Religious Society of Friends (Quakers) and Church of Scotland signed a 'Letter of Companionship'. Since then ecumenical co-operation has continued apace, including the creation of a Social Responsibility Forum and a Living Lightly programme for care of the environment. In 2018, an impressive Easter season mission entitled 'Moving Mountains' hit the national headlines.

Of course this initiative remains constrained by the historic differences which still separate the churches concerned. However, I believe that the way to resolve these differences lies in the passion and power of the people of God working together for the coming of the kingdom community, and in that process, affirming and developing what is most diaconal in each church. The future does *not* lie in trying to square a theological and ecclesiological circle in a retrograde and divisive way.

August 2018

Appendix[1]

'Communal holiness' and the kingdom community

'The Wesleyan movement was a commitment to a holiness project' (McMaster, 2002). In interpreting the nature of that project, Wesley knew that holiness, though a profoundly significant hallmark of the Christian life, must 'never (be) understood as an individualistic affair'. He declared that 'the gospel of Christ knows no religion but social: no holiness but social holiness' (*Called to Love and Praise*, 4.3.9). It should be remembered that Wesley was here setting the word 'social' over against the term 'solitary', and referring to how Christians should help one another to grow in the faith, not least as members of a class meeting. He was not here specifically concerned with the pursuit of social justice. Nevertheless, as McMaster argues, 'Today social holiness needs to be extended beyond ecclesial *koinonia*'.

My conviction is that if the concept of social holiness is taken into and 'extended' to become that of 'communal holiness', it takes on a radically new dimension and has the potential to become the gospel for our time.

There are a number of reasons why Methodism should (re)-embrace the concept of communal holiness. First, the Methodist Church needs to reclaim its holiness heritage and deflect David Hempton's criticism that Methodism lost its way when, by default, it relinquished this calling to 'its Holiness offspring ... Pentecostalism' (2005, pp. 208–209). Secondly, by 'extending social holiness beyond ecclesial *koinonia*', and enabling it to take on the mantle of communal holiness, we ground Methodism's holiness project in both the sociology and theology of *community*. This development would enable Methodism to make a uniquely important contribution to a world facing a choice between chaos and community. Its mission could then be seen as a call to build a global community of communities transformed by the gift of communal holiness.

---

[1] This Appendix is taken from Clark (2010) *Reshaping the Mission of Methodism*, pp. 172-180

This approach to the mission of Methodism raises two important questions. First, what do the concept of the kingdom community, which lies at the heart of the mission of the diaconal church, and the concept of communal holiness, have *in common*? Secondly, is there a *distinctive* contribution that the concept of communal holiness makes to our understanding of the mission of the diaconal church? I look at these two questions in turn.

1 The kingdom community and communal holiness – common ground

The concepts of communal holiness and the kingdom community share some key features in common. Both include 'community' as a foundational word. Thus anything learnt from religious or 'secular' disciplines about the nature of community will help to inform and enrich our understanding of the concepts of kingdom community and communal holiness.

Kingdom community and communal holiness are both means of grace. The gifts they bestow are neither a reward for effort, nor for good conduct. They are offered to humankind simply because God loves the world which he has created. They can be either refused, or accepted and used in the service of humankind.

The kingdom community and communal holiness both derive their transforming power from that of the Trinity. It should be remembered that the Trinity was one of 'the essential doctrines on which (Wesley) insisted' (Williams, 1960, p. 17). It is also of note that, since the 1980s, references to the doctrine of the Trinity have come increasingly to the fore in reports commissioned by the Methodist Conference (Shier-Jones in Marsh, et al., 2004, p. 86).

Called to Love and Praise (1.4.1) sees the communal nature of Trinity and kingdom as closely related. It comments: 'The synoptic gospels' understanding of the kingdom of God, and the Trinitarian understanding of God, implicit in the New Testament and developed in subsequent tradition, show how the church is a community both of worship and mission'. Complementing the communal attributes connecting kingdom and Trinity, Howard Snyder (2007) believes that the communal characteristics of holiness and Trinity are, likewise, closely linked. He writes: 'Mind-blowing as it sounds, holiness means sharing the very character of God – communion with the Trinity ... (Thus) Christians are to be specialists in building community to the glory of God' (pp. 74, 78).

The gifts of the kingdom community (life, liberation, love and learning) and the gift of communal holiness are gifts of the Trinity and reflect the latter's essentially communal nature (Clark, 2005, pp. 21–27, 37–40). However, the gift of communal holiness embodies and deepens our understanding of the gifts of the kingdom community as follows:

o The kingdom community's gift of *life* reflects the nature of God as Creator. It is a gift whose meaning is encapsulated in the phrase 'the glory of God is human beings fully alive' (Irenaeus).

For Wesley, this gift was that which enables men and women to become part of 'a new creation' (Wilkinson, 2004, p. 150–1). That creation is holy, or, as I shall argue later, a creation made whole. It brings into being a holy people eager to celebrate life in all its fullness. It calls them to worship, to thanksgiving, to service and to stewardship of the planet of which they are an integral part. Wesley preached and wrote much about individual responsibility in this connection. However, as Margaret Jones (2004) puts it, 'Holiness is the fruit of responsible grace in both the private and public spheres' (p. 161).

o The second gift of the kingdom community is *liberation*, both personal and collective. It is a gift manifest in the work of Christ as Liberator. Through this gift, we are freed *from* self, fear and a sense of failure. We are thus privileged, with the whole of creation, *to* experience the glorious liberty of the children of God (Romans 8: 21).

This gift is also a key feature of communal holiness. David Carter (2002) writes: Methodism's 'experience of salvation (holiness) is at one and the same time intensely personal and totally corporate' (p. 4). Personal liberation is the process of being made whole, forgiven and restored to our true selves through the grace of the liberating Christ. This experience of salvation, or 'healing holiness' as Jane Craske calls it (1999a, p. 178), is offered to each and all. Liberation is also about the redemption of the entire creation and encompasses the cosmic nature of communal holiness.

o   The third gift of the kingdom community is divine *love*, or *agape*. It is a gift which enables us to share the unity, or fellowship of the Holy Spirit. It is a gift that has a profound affinity with communal holiness.

It is through 'love divine, all loves excelling' that we receive the promise of becoming 'pure and spotless' and of being 'changed from glory into glory' (Charles Wesley). It is the 'Wesleyan emphasis on holiness as perfect love (that gives) Methodist spirituality its own distinctive character' and expresses 'the heart of Methodist ecclesiology' (*Called to Love and Praise*, 4.3.9; 4.3.10), a view echoed by Dion Forster in his endorsement of Methodism as a world faith (2009, p. 146). As Snyder (2007) puts it, 'Holiness … is not first of all a doctrine but … a love relationship with God in Jesus Christ and the Holy Spirit' (p. 82).

o   The fourth gift of the kingdom community is *learning*. It reflects what I believe is the nature of the Trinity as a learning community (Clark, 2005, pp. 37–38). This gift is a vital aspect of our search for communal holiness and summons us to an ongoing journey of spiritual discovery and growth.

Stephen Dawes (2003) writes, 'It is a journey from new birth to spiritual maturity, from sinfulness to perfection, from "original sin" through "justification by faith" to "entire sanctification".' Or as Wesley might have put it, learning is the journey towards perfect love. It is a gift which requires the people called Methodists to become 'a community of seekers' (David Deeks, Team Focus, p. 5) rather than those who never move beyond what they have received from their forebears. It also requires that they are open to engage with those whom Curran calls 'questers' (2009a, p. 109), seekers in the wider world.

In these ways, the gift of communal holiness embodies and enriches our understanding of the gifts of the kingdom community, the '4Ls'.

The four gifts of the kingdom community and the gift of communal holiness are universal and inclusive. They are yet to come in all their fullness, but are already among us, not only within the church but throughout our world. The mission of the diaconal church is to discern, make known and enable the gifts of the kingdom community, embodied in the gift of communal holiness, to bear fruit wherever they are found.

The universality of these gifts is reflected in Wesley's Arminianism, or 'the vision of "allness"', as Richard Andrew calls it (1999, p. 22). Methodism's 'special vocation within the universal church,' Andrew adds, is to push 'the logic of "catholicity" in the direction of its widest possible focus, the unity (and, we would add, the holiness) of *all* humanity' (p. 22). Such a world is an 'ecumenical' world, in the fullest and richest sense of an often misunderstood and narrowly defined concept.

The gift of communal holiness embodies and enriches our understanding of the four gifts of the kingdom community. However, the concept of communal holiness also offers a *distinctive* contribution to our understanding of those gifts, in particular their relationship to one another.

2 The kingdom community and communal holiness – the distinctive contribution of communal holiness

Informing the distinctiveness of the gift of communal holiness is a theology of integrity. This sees 'holiness' as 'wholeness', in the fullest and deepest sense of the latter word. As Jane Craske comments, holiness, coming from the same Germanic root as wholeness, links to a range of concepts 'about healing, being complete, having integrity' (1999a, p. 178). Thus I offer the following definition.

> *Communal holiness is that divine gift which, embodying the kingdom community's gifts of life, liberation, love and learning, transforms humankind into whole persons, whole families, whole institutions, whole cities, whole societies and one world, and points towards the integrity of creation.*

Holiness as wholeness is about 'the call to personhood' (McFadyen, 1990). It is about individuals, families, social collectives, cities, societies and humankind becoming, by divine grace, what God intended them to be (Clutterbuck, 2004, p. 68). Holiness as wholeness is also about the entire cosmos made whole, 'the integrity of creation' as the

145

World Council of Churches held at Seoul, 1990, describes it. In short, communal holiness as communal wholeness is about our human and divine destiny.

Because communal holiness is a unifying concept, it *integrates* the kingdom community's gifts of life, liberation, love and learning. It enables us to see that the gift of life which energises us, the gift of liberation which redeems us, the gift of love which bonds us, and the gift of learning which enables us to grow and develop, are complementary gifts which, by God's grace and human endeavour, empower humankind to become whole.

Holiness as wholeness does not mean homogeneity. As a gift rooted in the nature of the Trinity, it affirms distinctiveness, though as an integral aspect of a profound unity. Holiness treasures the riches of diversity, though it is a diversity that affirms interdependence. It embraces difference, sometimes disagreement and even conflict, but as human exchanges. These can open up new horizons and give impetus to humankind's quest to build a society and world which are communally whole.

The gift of communal holiness knows no divide between the 'sacred' and 'secular'. Consequently the mission of the diaconal church involves building partnerships with those embracing other faiths and other convictions who are striving to build communities that manifest the gift of communal holiness, whether or not that gift is recognised or acknowledged as such by them.

The gift of communal holiness is offered to a world that is unholy, is far from whole. It is offered to a world that is divided, fragmented, broken and at war with itself, because of humankind's inhumanity, greed, arrogance and selfishness. The failure of individuals and collectives to accept the gift of communal holiness, and the gifts of life, liberation, love and learning which it embodies, exposes the destructive power of all that is unholy. The result is that, though communal holiness reveals the immensity of God's grace, it is a gift that comes at a price to both Giver and receiver. To bestow that gift meant a self-emptying and cross for the Giver; to receive that gift means, for us, taking up our cross and following him. As the title of a Methodist consultation held in 2009 reminds us, 'holiness and risk' are inseparable.

3 Communal virtues and beyond

The gift of communal holiness, which embraces and unifies the gifts of life, liberation, love and learning, is a theological concept. If such a concept is to have any impact on everyday life, personal or corporate, it will need to be translated into more practical expressions of holiness. A useful bridge between a theological understanding and practical expressions of communal holiness is the concept of 'virtue ethics'.

The concept of 'virtue ethics' has a long and complex history (Macintyre, 1985). However, for our purposes, I define 'virtues' as those qualities which, when expressed in action, lead towards our human and divine destiny as whole persons and whole collectives. I also describe such virtues as 'communal'. This is because they connect the gift of communal holiness with the activities and relationships of daily life. Communal virtues are what, in ethical terms, go to make up what is often described as the common or, as I would put it, the communal good.

Identifying the communal virtues that give practical expression to communal holiness, and thus the '4Ls' it embodies, requires continuing theological and ethical research and reflection. However, some communal virtues appear to be more closely associated than others with one of the '4Ls', though there is inevitably a good deal of overlap. For example:

- o the gift of *life* could be said to encompass such communal virtues as creativity, beauty, well-being, enjoyment, gratitude and thanksgiving;
- o the gift of *liberation* might embrace the virtues of forgiveness, reconciliation, hope, fulfillment, justice and peace;
- o the gift of *love* might be expressed through the virtues of compassion, caring, sharing, friendship, trust, loyalty, honesty, generosity and equality;
- o the gift of *learning* might be seen as embracing the virtues of humility, openness, imagination, insight, perseverance and wisdom.

One problem in claiming that communal holiness gives expression to these communal virtues is that our post-modern world appears have lost any sense of a shared *telos*. Thus there is 'an inability to agree upon a catalogue of the virtues and an even more fundamental inability to agree upon the relative importance of the virtue concepts within a moral scheme', writes Alastair MacIntyre (p. 244). If this is the case, the concepts of communal holiness, of the '4Ls' and of the communal virtues, are going to carry little meaning, and less weight, simply as abstract ideas. Consequently, as MacIntyre argues, 'What matters at this stage (in human history) is *the construction of local forms of community* (my italics) within which civility and the intellectual and moral life can be sustained through the new dark ages which are already upon us' (p. 263).

The implications for us are that for the communal virtues to be understood, appreciated and sustained, they must be embodied within, what Stanley Hauerwas (1981) calls, 'communities of character'. Consequently, a mission strategy committed to offering the gift of communal holiness to humankind will only have credibility if the medium becomes the message. In short, mission as the task of the building a communally whole society and world cannot even start, let alone be accomplished, unless the universal church and not least Methodism, with its special call to witness to the gift of communal holiness, demonstrate through their own life and work, what communal wholeness is all about

18 theses for a renewed diaconate

1. A renewed diaconate is a gift of God to the church to come.
2. The nature and form of a renewed diaconate is founded on a kingdom theology and diaconal ecclesiology.
3. A renewed diaconate is a hall-mark of the diaconal church.
4. A renewed diaconate is an order of ministry.
5. The primary calling of a renewed diaconate is that of mission enablers. Thus it can also be designated as an order of mission.
6. As mission enablers, the role of a renewed diaconate is to equip the people of God for their ministry of kingdom community building in the world.
7. A renewed diaconate represents the church as a movement for the communal transformation of society and world.
8. A renewed diaconate is a religious order bonded by a shared calling and common discipline.
9. A renewed diaconate is a life-long calling.
10. A renewed diaconate is made up of women and men, single and married, paid and self-supporting.
11. A renewed diaconate exercises servant leadership.
12. A renewed diaconate is a full and equal order of ministry alongside presbyters (priests) and bishops.
13. Members of a renewed diaconate may be appointed to any position of leadership within the church.
14. Members of a renewed diaconate have a distinctive part to play in the conduct of worship, especially where this is focused on equipping the people of God for their ministry in the world.
15. Members of a renewed diaconate are authorized to preside at holy communion and other sacraments as and when the situation is related to their calling as an order of mission.
16. The selection and training of a renewed diaconate reflects the distinctiveness of its calling as an order of mission and its life as a religious order.
17. Within the diaconal church, it is open for presbyters, who feel so called, to become deacons and for deacons, who feel so called, to become presbyters.
18. A renewed diaconate may be supported by a diaconal lay 'third order'.

18 theses for the diaconal church[1]

1. In the millennium ahead, our world faces a choice between chaos and community.
2. If it is to survive, human civilization has to choose to become a global community of communities, ranging from micro communities (the family) to macro communities (major institutions and nation states).
3. The Christian vision of 'the kingdom community' is the supreme exemplification of all communities, and thus a model for world and church.
4. The gifts of the kingdom community are life, liberation, love and learning. They are gifts manifest within the nature of the Trinity and in Christ's teaching about the kingdom of God. They are universal gifts offered to all.
5. The mission of the church is to model and to build communities that are transformed by and manifest the gifts of the kingdom community. The credibility and viability of the church depends on how faithfully it fulfils this mission.
6. Such a mission can only be fulfilled if the church becomes a 'diaconal' (servant) church. The diaconal church is the servant of the kingdom community and of humankind. As such it models for both church and world what it means to be a human community.
7. The diaconal church respects the autonomy of a secular culture but rejects the domination of sacralism or secularism.
8. The social collectives that make up the diaconal church – hearings, groups, networks, the institution as an entity and partnerships – are all communal collectives.
9. Dialogue is fundamental to the means by which the diaconal church communicates its message.
10. The diaconal church liberates its laity to build communities that are transformed by the gifts of the kingdom community.
11. The diaconal church has two main forms:

---

[1] For a full description of the nature of the diaconal church see Clark (2005 and 2008)

- as the Christian community gathered for worship, learning and caring;
- as the Christian community dispersed to fulfil its mission in the world.
12. To equip the laity to be the servants of the kingdom community new forms of church leadership are needed. These are embodied in the roles of 'servant leader' and 'mission enabler'. The latter necessitates leaders being trained to equip lay people to become community builders within church and world.
13. Leaders of the diaconal church are women and men, married or single, paid or self-supporting.
14. The leadership of the diaconal church is exercised through three 'full and equal' orders of ministry:
    - that of 'presbyter' – whose task is to equip the gathered church to model the kingdom community in its life and work;
    - that of 'deacon' – whose task is to equip the dispersed church to build communities that manifest the gifts of the kingdom community in the world;
    - that of 'bishop' – whose task is to be an intermediary who supports and resources presbyters and deacons and, through them, the laity.
15. The diaconal church embraces a collective form of church leadership.
16. Within the diaconal church all work collaboratively.
17. The diaconal church is a democratic and self-governing church, based on the principle of subsidiarity.
18. For the diaconal church to fulfil its mission, the mould of Christendom must be broken.

Bibliography

Andrew, R. 'An impoverished catholicity: Theological considerations for a Methodist future' in, Craske, J. and Marsh, C. (eds.) (1999) *Methodism and the Future*. London: Cassell

Arias, M. (1984) *Announcing the Reign of God*. Philadelphia: Fortress

Atkins, M. (2007) *Resourcing Renewal: Shaping churches for the emerging future*. Peterborough: Inspire

Avis, P. (2013) 'The Diaconate: a flagship ministry?' in *Theology and Ministry* 2.1

Baptism, Eucharist and Ministry (1982). Geneva: World Council of Churches, Faith and Order

Barnett, J.M. (1995) (third edition) *The Diaconate: A Full and Equal Order*. Harrisburg, PA: Trinity Press

Borgegard, G., Fanuelsen, O. and Hall, C. (eds.) (1999) *The Ministry of the Deacon*,
1. *Anglican-Lutheran Perspectives*. Uppsala: Nordic Ecumenical Council.

Borgegard, G., Fanuelsen, O. and Hall, C. (eds.) (2000) *The Ministry of the Deacon*,
2. *Ecclesiological Explorations*. Uppsala: Nordic Ecumenical Council

Brown, R. (2005) *The Ministry of the Deacon*. Norwich: Canterbury Press

Called to Love and Praise: A Methodist Conference Statement on the Church (1999) Peterborough: Methodist Publishing House

Carter, D. (2002) *Love Bade Me Welcome. A British Methodist perspective on the Church*. London: Epworth Press

Clark, D. (May 1974) 'The Church as Symbolic Place' in *Epworth Review*, Vol 1, No 2 London: Methodist Publishing House or from david@clark58.eclipse.co.uk

Clark, D. (1977) *Basic Communities*. London: SPCK

Clark, D. (1984) *The Liberation of the Church*. Westhill College, Birmingham: NACCCAN

Clark, D. (1987) *Yes to Life*. London: Collins

Clark, D. (1988) *What Future for Methodism?* Birmingham: Harborne
    Group
Clark, D. (1996) *Schools as Learning Communities*. London: Cassell
Clark, D. (1997) *Changing World, Unchanging Church?* London:
    Mowbray
Clark, D. (2004) 'Mission in a Society without God' in *Crucible*. April
    – July 2004. Lowestoft: Tyndale Press
Clark, D. (2005; second printing 2014) *Breaking the Mould of
    Christendom: Kingdom community, diaconal church and the liberation of the
    laity*. Peterborough: Upfront Publishing
Clark, D. (ed.) (2008) *The Diaconal Church – beyond the mould of
    Christendom*. Peterborough: Epworth Press
Clark, D. (November 2008) *The Formation and Training of Deacons*.
    Birmingham: Methodist Diaconal Order. Available from – david@
    clark58.eclipse.co.uk
Clark, D. (2010) *Reshaping the mission of Methodism – a diaconal church
    approach*. Oldham: Church in the Market Place
Clark, D. (2012) *Building the Human City – the Origins and Future
    Potential of the Human City Institute (1995 – 2002)*. Birmingham:
    Human City Institute (available from HCI, 239 Holliday Street,
    Birmingham B1 1SJ or download from www.humancity.org.uk)
Clark, D. (2013) 'The hallmark of the Methodist Diaconal Order –
    its life as a religious order – and some implications the future of
    Methodism' in *Theology and Ministry – An Online Journal*. (Vol. 2)
    University of Durham: St John's College – www.durham.ac.uk/
    theologyandministry
Clark, D. (2014) *The Kingdom at Work Project – a communal approach to
    mission in the workplace*. Peterborough: Upfront Publishing
Clark, D. (2016) *Building Kingdom Communities – with the diaconate as a
    new order of mission*. Peterborough: Fast-print Publishing
Clark, D. (September, 2016) *A critique of the Faith and Order Committee's
    Interim Report on the place of the diaconate within Methodism and the
    universal church*. (unpublished paper – available from david@clark58.
    eclipse.co.uk)
Clutterbuck, R. 'Theology as Interaction: Ecumenism and the World
    Church' in Marsh, C., Beck, B., Shier-Jones, A. and Wareing, H.
    (eds.) (2004) *Unmasking Methodist Theology*. London: Continuum

Collins, J. N. (1990) *Diakonia: Re-interpreting the Ancient Sources.* Oxford: Oxford University Press

Collins, J. N. (1992) *Are All Christians Ministers?* Newtown, Australia: E. J. Dwyer

Collins, J. N. (2002) *Deacons and the Church.* Leominster: Gracewing

Collins, J.N. (2014) *Diakonia Studies: Critical issues in ministry.* Oxford: Oxford University Press

Craske, J. and Marsh, C. (1999) *Methodism and the Future.* London: Cassell

Craske, J. 'The threads with which we weave: Towards a holy church' in Craske, J. and Marsh, C. (eds.) (1999a) *Methodism and the Future.* London: Cassell

Croft, S. (1999) *Ministry in Three Dimensions.* London: Darton, Longman and Todd

Curran, L. and Shier-Jones, A. (2009) *Methodist Present Potential.* Peterborough: Epworth

Curran, L. 'A Shared Faith' (2009a) in Curran, L. and Shier-Jones, A. *Methodist Present Potential.* Peterborough: Epworth

Dare to be a deacon (2009-2010) London: Methodist Publishing

Dawes. S. (2003) 'The Spirituality of "Scriptural Holiness" '. Scriptural Holiness Project: www.methodist.org.uk

Deacons of the Gospel – A Vision for Today : A Ministry for Tomorrow (2000) Church of Scotland

Deacons of Word and Service – the vision statement of the Church of Scotland diaconate (2018)

DIAKONIA. The World Federation of Diaconal Associations and Communities (for legal purposes domiciled in the Netherlands) – www.diakonia-world.org

Diakonia – Challenge and Response (1996) The Netherlands: World Federation of Diaconal Associations and Communities

The Distinctive Diaconate (2003). Salisbury: Diocese of Salisbury

Ditewig, W. T. (2007) *The Emerging Diaconate – Servant Leaders in a Servant Church.* New York/Mahwah, NJ: Paulist Press

Elliott, C. (1985) *Praying the Kingdom.* London: Darton, Longman and Todd)

Epting, S. W. (2015) *Unexpected Consequences – The Diaconate Renewed.* New York: Morehouse Publishing

Forster, D. 'A world faith' in Curran, L. and Shier-Jones, A. (eds.)
(2009) *Methodist Present Potential*. Peterborough: Epworth Press

For such a time as this. A renewed diaconate in the Church of England (2001).
London: Church House Publishing

Fowler, J. 'The contribution of the Methodist Diaconal Order to the
ministry and mission of the future church' in Clark, D. (ed.) (2010)
Reshaping the mission of Methodism. Oldham: Church in the Market
Place

From the Diakonia of Christ to the Diakonia of the Apostles (2003).
International Theological Commission. London: Catholic Truth
Society

Gibbs, M. and Morton, T. R. (1964) *God's Frozen People*. London:
Fontana/Collins

Gibbs, M. and Morton, T. R. (1971) *God's Lively People*. London:
Fontana/Collins

The Gift of Connexionalism in the 21st Century. Report to the Methodist
Conference, 2017

Graham, E. D. (2002) *Saved to Serve. The Story of the Wesley Deaconess
Order. 1890-1978*. Peterborough: Methodist Publishing House

Greenleaf, R. K. (1970). *The Servant as Leader* (numerous publishers)

The Hanover Report, *The Diaconate as Ecumenical Opportunity* (1996).
Report of the Anglican-Lutheran International Commission.
Anglican Communion Publications

Hauerwas, S. (1981) *A Community of Character*. South Bend, IN:
University of Notre Dame Press

Hempton, D. (2005) *Methodism – Empire of the Spirit*. New Haven and
London: Yale University Press

Hull, J. M. (1985) *What Prevents Christian Adults from Learning?* London:
SCM Press

Hull, J. M. (1993) *The Hockerill Lecture. 1993*. London: Hockerill
Educational Foundation

In the Navy... (2011-2012) London: Methodist Publishing House

Interim Report (2016) *The Theology and Ecclesiology Underpinning the
Diaconate – 2016*. Methodist Church Faith and Order Committee
report to the Methodist Conference
www.methodist.org.uk/.../conf-2016-33-Theology-and-
Eccesiology-underpinning-the- Diaconate

Into All the World: Being and Becoming Apostolic Churches (2014) A report to the Anglican Consultative Council and the World Methodist Council. Anglican-Methodist International Commission for Unity in Mission (AMICUM)

The Iona Report – The Diaconate in the Anglican Church of Canada (2016). The General Synod of the Anglican Church of Canada

Jackson, D. M. (2018, revised) *The Diaconate Renewed: Service, Word and Worship.* Diocese of Qu'Appelle, Anglican Church of Canada. Download from: https://quappelle.anglican.ca/assets/.../The_ Diaconate_Renewed-November_2015.pdf

Jackson, S. 'The Methodist Diaconal Order: a sign of the diaconal church' in Clark, D. (ed.) (2008) *The Diaconal Church: Beyond the Mould of Christendom.* Peterborough: Epworth Press

The Jerusalem Report (2012). *To Love and Serve the Lord – Diakonia in the Life of the Church.* Report of the Anglican-Lutheran International Commission (ALIC III)

Jones, M. 'Growing in Grace and Holiness' in Marsh, C. et al. (2004) *Unmasking Methodist Theology.* London: Continuum

Kingdom at Work Project Bulletin – download from: http://www. saltleytrust.org.uk/faith-and-work-in-theological-education-and-training/

Lambert, L. (1999) *Called to Serve.* Manual for the Diaconate. Evangelical Lutheran Church in America, 8765 West Higgins Road, Chicago IL 60631, USA

Lloyd, J. M. (2010) *Women and the Shaping of British Methodism: Persistent Preachers, 1807-1907.* Manchester and New York: Manchester University Press

MacIntyre, A. (1985) (2nd edn.) *After Virtue: A study in moral theory.* London: Duckworth

McMaster, J. (2002) 'Wesley on Social Holiness'. Scriptural Holiness Project. www.methodist.org.uk

Marsh, C., Beck, B., Shier-Jones, A. and Wareing, H. (eds.) (2004) *Unmasking Methodist Theology.* London: Continuu1m

Martin, D. (2016) *Ruin and Restoration.* London: Routledge

McFadyen, A. L. (1990) *The Call to Personhood.* Cambridge: Cambridge University Press

Mead, L. B. (1991) *The One and Future Church.* New York: The Alban Institute.

Methodist Council Paper MC/13/13 *Review of the Role of the Warden of the Methodist Diaconal Order,* Recommendation 1

Methodist Deed of Union, 1932, Section 2, Clause 4

Methodist Faith and Order Committee (working party), Interim Report (2016). www.methodist.org.uk/.../33-theology-and-ecclesiology-underpinning-the-diaconate

Ministerial Code of Conduct (2016) Methodist Conference report. www.methodist.org.uk/.../counc-mc17-18-ministerial-code-of-conduct-january-2017

The Ministry of the People of God. Methodist Conference (1988)

The Ministry of the People of God in the World. Methodist Conference (1990)

Mission and Ministry in Covenant (2018) A report from the Faith and Order bodies of the Church of England and the Methodist Church www.churchofengland.org/sites/default/.../mission-and-ministry-in-covenant.pdf

The Mission and Ministry of the Whole Church (2007). London: Church House Publishing

mission-shaped church (2004). London: Church House Publishing

Newcome, J. (2018) *The Diaconate – Renewing an Ancient Ministry.* Download from www.deaconstories.wordpress.com/about/

O'Loughlin, T. (2015) *Washing Feet – imitating the example of Jesus in the liturgy today.* Minnesota: Liturgical Press

Orton, A. and Stockdale, T. (2014) *Making Connections – Exploring Methodist Deacons' Perspectives on Contemporary Diaconal Ministry.* Durham: Sacristy Press

Shier-Jones, A. 'Pioneering Circuit Ministry' in *Epworth Review* (July 2009) Vol. 36. No. 3. London: Methodist Publishing'

Shreeve, E. and Luscombe, P. (2002) *What is a Minister?* Peterborough: Epworth Press

Singing the Faith (2011) London: Hymns Ancient & Modern

Snyder, H. A. 'Holiness of heart and life in a post-modern world' in Greenway, J.B. and Green, J. B (2007) *Grace and Holiness in a Changing World.* Nashville: Abingdon Press

Staton, M. W. (2000) *Biblical and Early Church Sources for Diaconal Ministry* (unpublished paper)

Staton, M. W. (2001) *The Development of the Diaconal Ministry in the Methodist Church: A Historical and Theological Study.* Ph.D. thesis (unpublished): University of Leeds

Staton, M. W. (2013) 'The Development of Diaconal Ministry in the Methodist Church in Britain' in *Theology and Ministry – An Online Journal*. (Vol. 2) University of Durham: St John's College – www.durham.ac.uk/theologyandministry

Underhill, E. (1953) *An Anthology of the Love of God*. London: Mowbray

Voices from the margins (2005) London: Methodist Church Communications Office

What is a Deacon? (2004) Methodist Conference Report

What is a Presbyter? (2002) Methodist Conference Report

Who do you say we are? (2010-2011) London: Methodist Publishing

The Windsor Statement of the United Kingdom Ecumenical Diaconal Consultation. (1997, October 1-3) Birmingham: Methodist Diaconal Order. Issued following a consultation between the Church of Scotland, the Scottish Episcopal Church, the British Methodist Church, the Roman Catholic Church and the Church of England. The consultation included conversations with a United Reformed Church CRCW and a Deacon in training in the Orthodox Church.

Wilkinson, D. 'The Activity of God in Methodist Perspective' in Marsh, C. et al. (2004) *Unmasking Methodist Theology*. London: Continuum

Williams, C. (1960) *John Wesley's Theology Today*. London: Epworth Press